TONY AND CLEO

PLAYS BY HOWARD RUBENSTEIN

AGAMEMNON by Aeschylus, translated with reconstructed stage directions

BRITANNICUS by Jean Racine, translated and adapted

BROTHERS ALL

THE GOLEM, MAN OF EARTH

TONY AND CLEO

THE TROJAN WOMEN by Euripides, translated and adapted in response to Aristophanes' and Aristotle's criticism of Euripides

TONY AND CLEO

A PLAY IN TWO ACTS

BY

HOWARD RUBENSTEIN

GRANITE HILLS PRESS™
SAN DIEGO

TONY and CLEO
A Play in Two Acts
by Howard Rubenstein

Published 2008 by Granite Hills Press™
SAN 298-072X

Cover by Chuck Conners, cyberwatercolor based on photographs by Paul Savage

Cataloging in Publication
Rubenstein, Howard S., 1931–
    Tony and Cleo : a play in two acts / by Howard Rubenstein ;
        p. cm
        LCCN: 2008931131
        ISBN-13: 978-1-929468-13-3
        ISBN-10: 1-929468-13-X
        1. Roman--Drama.   2. Historical--Drama.   3. Romance--
            Drama.
    I. Plutarch ; Cicero.
    II. Title.

Printed in the United States of America

To Judy

ACKNOWLEDGMENTS

Many people helped realize the play *Tony and Cleo*—the script, the production, and the published book. The play is historical fiction, and my principal sources were Plutarch's *Life of Marcus Antonius*; Cicero's *Philippic Orations*, especially the *Second*; Velleius Paterculus's *History of Rome*; and *The Accomplishments of the Divine Augustus* (autobiography). Lesser but also important sources included Latin poems by Horace, Catullus, Martial, and Vergil, and Dryden's play *All for Love*.

Tony and Cleo had its premiere at 6th@Penn Theatre, San Diego, on February 3, 2008, produced by Dale Morris and directed by Tyler Richards Hewes. Stage manager was Anna Ashmore; costume designer, Abigail Hewes; and choreographer, Lesha Montoya. The cast comprised Richard Carrillo (Tony), Lesha Montoya (Cleo), Anthony Hamm (Eros), Joseph Baker (Octavian Caesar/Cornelius), Melissa Coleman Reed (Avia), Tyler Herdklotz (Ventidius/Canidius), and Jennie Olson (Charmion).

I am grateful to the director and cast for suggesting changes to clarify and improve the script. I thank Ingar Quist for editing the final drafts of the book. Finally, I am most grateful to my wife, Judy, not only for her critical editing and many helpful suggestions but also, and especially, for her love, support, and encouragement.

Howard Rubenstein
San Diego
August 8, 2008

TIME LINE

44 BCE Marcus Antonius (MA; Tony in the play) meets Cleopatra (C; Cleo in the play) in Rome while he and Julius Caesar (JC) are co-consuls. (The exact year of their meeting is unknown.) JC is assassinated by the defenders of the Roman Republic led by Brutus and Cassius. JC's nineteen-year-old nephew and principal heir, Octavian, becomes JC's adopted son and assumes the family name Caesar, becoming Octavian Caesar (OC). Largely through the persuasion of the statesman and orator Cicero, Rome turns against MA and toward OC, who succeeds MA and JC as sole consul and takes control of the Roman army. MA flees Rome to northern Italy.

43 BCE OC defeats MA and his ally Marcus Aemilius Lepidus in northern Italy. OC reconciles with them, and the three form the second triumvirate (43–33 BCE).

42 BCE MA and OC track down Brutus and Cassius, the leading assassins of JC and the last defenders of liberty, at Philippi, Macedonia. MA defeats them, whereupon Brutus and Cassius commit suicide. MA's victory is the coup de grace to the Roman Republic. MA celebrates his victory throughout all Greece and makes his home in Athens.

41 BCE MA orders C to meet him at Tarsus on the Cydnus, Cilicia (Turkey), to defend herself against the rumor that she supported Brutus and Cassius at Philippi.

40 BCE OC and MA partition the Mediterranean along the Ionian Sea, with OC getting the western half—Italy, Gaul, and the Iberian Peninsula; MA, the eastern half—Greece and "Asia" (today's Middle East and called that in the play); and Lepidus, a segment of the north coast of Africa. MA marries OC's favorite sister, Octavia (Avia in the play), in Rome, and they settle in MA's home in Athens. MA sends General Ventidius to Syria, a Roman province, to drive the aggressive Parthians out. (The Parthian Empire included modern-day Iraq, Iran, Afghanistan, and Pakistan.)

37 BCE Ventidius succeeds in driving the Parthians from Syria. MA invades the Parthian Empire, intent on making it a Roman province.

35 BCE MA is defeated by Parthia, and C persuades him to return with her to Alexandria.

32 BCE MA evicts Octavia from his home in Rome (tantamount to divorce) and makes the "Donations of Alexandria," giving all the eastern provinces to C and her descendants.

31 BCE OC and the Senate and the People of Rome (SPQR) strip MA of all power and declare war on C. OC defeats MA and C at the battle of Actium.

30 BCE OC defeats MA and C at the battle of Alexandria. MA and C commit suicide. OC makes Egypt a Roman province and reclaims for Rome the other eastern provinces. OC is now the unopposed and sole ruler of Rome.

27 BCE The Roman provinces are henceforth called the Roman Empire, and OC is its first emperor. SPQR changes OC's name to Augustus, a religious title meaning Sacred or Revered or Divine, and he is declared a god (perhaps as early as 29 BCE). A temple to Augustus is erected, and priests conduct sacred rites devoted to him.

The cult of Augustus existed until the fourth century CE, when the emperors Constantine and, especially, Theodosius abolished it along with the ancient Roman religion and made Christianity the state religion of Rome.

TONY AND CLEO

CHARACTERS

TONY (Marcus Antonius, Mark Antony, Mark, Antony), Roman commander. A ruggedly good-looking man, athletic, in his late thirties in 44 BCE.

CLEO (Cleopatra), queen of Egypt. A woman of unusual beauty, in her midtwenties in 44 BCE.

EROS, Tony's aide. In his twenties or thirties in 44 BCE.

OCTAVIAN (Caesar, Octavian Caesar), nephew and adopted son of Julius Caesar. Handsome, boyish, athletic, aged nineteen in 44 BCE.

AVIA (Octavia), Octavian Caesar's sister. A pretty woman, refined, in her twenties in 44 BCE.

VENTIDIUS, Tony's general in Syria. Athletic, in his forties.

CANIDIUS, Tony's general at Actium. Athletic, in his forties.

CHARMION, Cleo's attendant. Attractive, in her twenties or thirties.

CORNELIUS, one of Tony's soldiers in Parthia, in his twenties.

Time: 44–30 BCE.

Places: Rome; Athens; Alexandria; Tarsus on the
Cydnus, Cilicia (modern-day Turkey); White Vil-
lage Harbor, Syria; a battlefield somewhere in the
Parthian Empire (includes modern-day Iraq, Iran,
Afghanistan, and Pakistan); Actium, Greece.

SCENES

PRELUDE

ACT I

INTERLUDE

ACT II

EPILOGUE

NOTES

Costumes are of the period.

Sets for a small theater are minimal. Colorful pillows and cushions on a sheet on the floor or on a platform may represent a bed, the sheet also serving to carry the pillows during set changes. A large cube may represent a stool or a platform or, covered with a cushion, a throne; two cubes, a bench; and six cubes, a platform for a bed. Colorful draperies may cover the walls. Two doors upstage as well as the center aisle may serve as entrances or exits.

Latin pronunciation: A coach of ancient Latin is needed for the actors who have Latin lines. The coach should make an exception in the case of the pronunciation of words containing the letter v for which the English pronunciation should be used. In Latin, v is pronounced like w; thus, the names Avia and Ventidius would sound like Awia and Wentidius, respectively, with the undesirable comic result of sounding like baby talk.

PRELUDE

A sensuous and ancient Egyptian-style dance accompanied by the music of drums, flute, lute, and tambourines.

(Fade-out.)

ACT I

Scene 1

30 BCE, Alexandria, Egypt, Tony's retreat.

EROS. (*Enters.*) The year is 30 BCE
    by modern reckoning.
    The place is Alexandria, Egypt.
    My name is Eros.
    I am the servant and aide
    of Marcus Antonius.
    He is also known as Mark Antony
    or Antony,
    and by a few intimates as Mark,
    and by a very few
    (*Proudly pointing to himself.*)
    as Tony. (*Pause.*)

7

Eros is the God of Love.
I am not well named.
Parents must be careful
about the names they give their children.
Eros is a primal god,
born before the Olympians—
before Zeus or Jupiter,
the Father of gods and men,
before Aphrodite or Venus,
the Goddess of Love.
Eros is the best looking of the gods.
(*Jokingly conceited.*) That part
of the god's description fits.
(*Serious.*) He is the irresistible
and unrelenting procreative force
of the universe.
Within the hearts of men and gods,
he weakens the limbs
and overcomes the mind,
conquering willpower, good judgment,
and common sense,

> (*Lighting now reveals* TONY, *bare
> chested, barefoot, despondent,
> stone-faced, sitting on the floor,
> head in hands.*)

but never so much as he did
where Marcus Antonius
was concerned. (*Pause.*)
Tony's love for Cleopatra
and hers for him
is a love that has no limits.

A love like that is a sickness.
It takes away all sense of duty
and responsibility.
Lovers like that are so high on love
that reason is beyond them
because they're lost
among the stars.

And as if one devastating illness
wasn't enough,
some god has recently inflicted him
with another—a deadly one—
the black midnight of the soul.

We are inside Tony's cabin
built on the breakwater
of Alexandria's harbor, his retreat.
He hasn't eaten or slept for days.
He refuses to see anyone except me.
He refuses to see even her.
He has descended into darkest thought,
blames himself for everything,
and talks constantly of death.

Let's see whether I can cheer him up.

(*Touching* TONY *on the shoulder.*)

TONY. Go away!

EROS. My lord, it's me, Eros.

TONY. Go away!

EROS. But I want to see you.

TONY. Now that you've seen me,
　　are you satisfied?

EROS. But I want to help you.

TONY. (*In despair.*) But you can't!
　　Don't you understand how I'm suffering?

EROS. Yes! And your suffering is mine!

TONY. I'm a good-for-nothing—
　　worthless, a loser!
　　I've led a life of debauchery,
　　and it's caught up with me.
　　(*Abrupt change in mood.*)
　　What happened at Actium?

EROS. Captain, we lost the battle.
　　We sailed away, confident of victory,
　　and then Octavian Caesar's fleet
　　set our boats afire
　　by shooting flaming arrows
　　and by hurling burning torches
　　onto the decks.
　　A strong wind fanned the flames
　　and stirred up giant waves.
　　Most of the ships sank,
　　and those that stayed afloat
　　Octavian Caesar captured.

TONY. So I lost the battle.

EROS. Everyone loses battles.
     Even Julius Caesar lost a few.

TONY. Yes, but when Julius Caesar
     lost a battle,
     he did so honorably.
     At Actium I fled.
     I abandoned my ships
     and deserted my men.
     (*Affectless, slowly.*)
     And now you tell me
     our fleet's been destroyed.

EROS. (*To himself.*) Eros,
     help this madman
     who has worked so hard
     to bring about his own destruction!

TONY. Oh, why go on living?

EROS. Captain, at Actium
     you thought your presence
     was a hindrance.
     Your leaving was purposeful.
     That's not desertion.

TONY. That might be true
     had we won.
     But we lost. (*Pause.*)
     What about the land battle?

EROS. There was no land battle.
    All your soldiers on the shore
    refused to believe
    you had abandoned them
    and had sailed away.
    They imagined
    you would suddenly appear—
    descend from heaven?
    emerge from the foam of the sea?—
    and lead them.
    And even after they were convinced
    that you had truly fled,
    they kept their battalions
    and companies intact
    for seven whole days
    in spite of the messages
    from Octavian Caesar
    telling them the facts
    and asking them to surrender.
    Not until all your officers to a man
    and your allies, too,
    ran over to Caesar,
    did the foot soldiers and cavalry
    give up and surrender.

TONY. And now I wait
    for Caesar to finish the job
    here in Alexandria.

EROS. We can still put up a fight
    and die honorably,
    which is better
    than being taken in chains to Rome.

TONY. If the sailors
       insist on fighting,
       I won't stop them.
       But let them choose their own captain.
       I'm not fit to lead them.
       Be sure to tell them I said that.
       And afterward
       return immediately to me.
       There's something here
       I need you to do.

EROS. Yes, my lord.

TONY. And I still don't want
       to see anyone,
       not even her.

EROS. But what do I say
       if I meet someone
       who wants to visit you?

TONY. Tell him there's a fig tree
       with abundant fruit
       and strong branches
       just outside my cabin.

EROS. What do you mean?

TONY. He may eat all the figs he likes . . .
       or he can hang himself!
       But he can't visit me!

EROS. Yes, Commander! (*Turning to go.*)

TONY. Eros!

EROS. (*Turning back.*) Yes, my lord?

TONY. I'm writing my epitaph.
    I've already written quite a few.
    Do you want to hear them?

EROS. Yes, my lord.

TONY. (*To the audience.*)
    "Antony's life of misery is done.
    He curses you—everyone!"

EROS. I don't like it.

TONY. How about this?
    "Beneath this stone
    lies a misanthrope.
    Revile him all you like, Visitor!
    Just move along! Go!"

EROS. I don't like that one either.

TONY. What about this?
    "Although Marcus Antonius was lewd,
    he had a first-rate mind.
    He fucked much and he fought little,
    but he was generous and he was kind."

EROS. (*Considering.*) Better!

TONY. All right, you may go.

                    (*Fade-out.*)

                    Scene 2

44 BCE, Rome, Cleo's apartments.

EROS. Tony wasn't always like this,
          thinking only of failure and death.
          He was once a happy man,
          the happiest on earth.
          Like the first time he met Cleopatra.
          She was in her twenties then
          and totally captivated him by her charm,
          the sweetness of her voice,
          her unusual beauty,
          and keen intelligence.

          Let's go back fourteen years
          to 44 BCE by modern reckoning.
          Cleopatra was in Rome.

               (*Trumpet fanfare. Fanfare here and
               subsequently marks the locale as
               Rome.*)

          She was the mistress of Julius Caesar.
          Caesar and Tony
          were co-consuls that year.
          A consul is a Roman head of state,

and usually there were two of them
ruling together.
Rome was still a republic,
based on liberty,
and two consuls provided
balance of power.

Cleopatra wanted to meet Tony.
You see, everyone was talking about him,
saying what a good soldier he was,
Caesar's favorite,
a womanizer, good-looking,
an extravagant gift giver, a squanderer,
a drunkard, debauched, dissolute . . .
and charmingly crude.

> (CLEOPATRA *enters with* CHAR-
> MION *behind her.* CLEOPATRA
> *promenades, displaying her beauti-*
> *ful figure, then sits on her throne.*
> CHARMION *adjusts* CLEOPA-
> TRA*'s dress and primps her hair;*
> *when* CHARMION *is satisfied, she*
> *stands aside.*)

Tony came to her apartments
one afternoon,
and she kept him waiting a whole hour,
as very important people like to do
to visitors. (*Exits.*)

> (TONY *enters, bows, and kneels*
> *before* CLEOPATRA.)

TONY. *Ave*, Cleopatra,
　　Queen of Egypt!
　　I am Marcus Antonius,
　　co-consul with Julius Caesar
　　and . . .

　　　　(*Kissing her hand.*)

　　your faithful servant.

CLEO. I know who you are,
　　Marcus Antonius.

　　　　(*Scrutinizing him admiringly.*)

　　Now I understand
　　why Caesar hasn't arranged for us
　　to meet sooner. (*Pause.*)
　　As co-consul,
　　you must be Caesar's equal.

TONY. (*Standing.*) No.
　　No one is Caesar's equal.
　　He has Cleopatra.

CLEO. (*Smiling, standing.*)
　　I detect some insolence
　　in your flattery.

TONY. I was hoping you'd hear
　　only the flattery.

CLEO. (*Abruptly.*) Never mind!
    There's a rumor
    I'd like you to confirm or dispel.

TONY. What is it?

CLEO. I've heard that Julius Caesar
    wants to be King of Rome.

TONY. No! It's not true!
    The word *king* to the Romans
    means despot, absolute ruler,
    crusher of liberty.
    Caesar is not a despot.
    He genuinely loves the Republic
    and the Roman people.
    In the provinces
    kings appointed by Rome
    are useful
    to keep the populace enslaved,
    but in Rome
    a king would be intolerable.

CLEO. Would the Romans kill a man
    who wanted to be king?

TONY. Yes, they'd kill him!
    In the provinces
    they would crucify him,
    and in Rome
    they would assassinate him.
    My lady, you ask
    all the right questions.

You certainly understand
Roman politics.

CLEO. If what you say is so,
    why would Caesar ever think
    of becoming king?

TONY. He doesn't!
    Those who hate him
    say he wants to be king,
    because they want him killed.
    Some even say he wants to rule Rome
    together with the Queen of Egypt.

CLEO. (*Laughing.*) With me?
    That's ridiculous!
    No Roman—least of all Julius Caesar—
    would ever marry an Egyptian.
    Besides, he already has a devoted wife.

TONY. You keep talking about Caesar.
    Are you in love with him?

CLEO. An impertinent question
    on a first meeting,
    don't you think?

TONY. No, I don't think so.
    You're his mistress.
    Who else can answer the question?

CLEO. (*Smiling.*) Cicero says
    you're audacious.

TONY. I hate Cicero!
    But you haven't answered the question.

CLEO. (*Sitting*.)
    Well, I admire Caesar.
    He's the kindest man I've ever known,
    and the only one
    who not only forgives his enemies
    but also bestows honors on them,
    giving them positions
    in his government.

TONY. And . . .
    he's the father of your little boy.

CLEO. I would do anything for Caesar.
    But I do not love him.

TONY. If the Romans should harm him,
    what would you do?

CLEO. I'd have to flee Italy.
    They'd come to kill me. (*Pause*.)
    But what about you?
    Do you love Caesar?

TONY. Yes.
    He's always been good to me.

CLEO. He certainly loves you.
    He speaks of you often
    and in glowing terms.

(She caresses his leg with her foot.)

TONY. I know.

CLEO. You *are* impertinent.

TONY. Yes.

CLEO. You'd do nothing
to bring Caesar down?

TONY. Why should I?
Caesar is my friend.
If his enemies killed him,
they'd kill me, too.

CLEO. *(Standing.)*
Well, Marcus Antonius,
this has been
a most illuminating meeting.

(TONY *kisses her hand.*   CLEO
smiles and speaks to CHARMION.)

Sidere pulchrior ille est.

TONY. What did you say?

CLEO. *(To* TONY.*)*
Sidere pulchrior ille est.
[He is more beautiful than a star.]

TONY. That's poetry!
    Your Latin is very good!

CLEO. And so is my Greek . . .
    and Arabic . . . and Aramaic . . . and . . .

TONY. No one's called me beautiful—
    not since I was a boy.

CLEO. I meant in the sense
    of rugged good looks.

>   (TONY *kisses her ardently. She
>   slaps his face.*)

TONY. (*Smiling.*) I was just thinking
    how beautiful *you* are . . .
    in an unusual way.

CLEO. (*Taking offense.*) Thank you!
    It is my mind
    most men find attractive!

>   (*She sits.* TONY *kisses her passion-
>   ately. She slaps his face, whereupon
>   he kisses her even more passion-
>   ately. Again she slaps him.*)

TONY. (*Smiling.*) I like your mind
    well enough,
    but I like your face and body, too.

(TONY *kneels. He kisses her hands.*
Then removing her sandals, he
grows ever more bold and passion-
ate. CLEO *affects displeasure. He*
quickly thrusts his head beneath her
gown and performs oral sex. She
murmurs and moans. Her cries of
pleasure grow ever louder, ending
in a deep sigh. He emerges, and
she slaps his face. Smiling, he
stands, lifts her in his arms, and
kisses her hard on the mouth,
whereupon she again slaps him,
and he laughs. He sets her on her
feet and kisses her again, long and
tenderly. She does not slap him.
This time she, too, laughs. The sex-
ual act here and subsequently is
suggestive and passionate but not
pornographic.)

CLEO. I suppose
   you're going to tell your friends
   what you did to the Queen of Egypt
   on your first meeting!

TONY. No, my lady,
   I'm not the kind to kiss and tell,
   particularly where Caesar's mistress
   is concerned!
   My queen, this has been
   an unforgettable first meeting.
   I am henceforth and forever your slave.

(*He kneels and kisses her hand.*)

CLEO. Marcus Antonius,
  I can't begin to tell you
  how much I'd like to return the favor.
  But it's quite impossible
  and completely unsafe now.
  Caesar is expected at any moment.

   (*A darting glance from* CLEO
   sends CHARMION *off.*)

TONY. (*Standing and good-naturedly pointing to
  his groin.*)
  Well, what is to be done about this?

CLEO. Come back tomorrow,
  and I'll take care of you.

TONY. Tomorrow! But I need relief today!

CLEO. Marcus Antonius,
  you know countless women
  who'd be honored
  to take care of you today.

   (*He grins.*)

  One last thing. I can hardly
  call you Marcus Antonius anymore.
  What do your friends call you?

TONY. Antony.

CLEO. I mean your dear friends.

TONY. Mark.

CLEO. Your *dearest* friends.

TONY. Tony.

CLEO. Mmm. (*Sounding.*) *Tony.*

TONY. And what do people call you?

CLEO. Cleopatra.

TONY. Yes. Everyone knows that!
    But what do your friends call you?

CLEO. I have no friends.

TONY. (*Chuckling.*) Well, then,
    I'll call you Cleopatra, too.
    (*Contemplating.*)
    No. What about . . . Cleo?

CLEO. *Cleo.*
    No one has ever called me that.
    Mmm. I rather like it.
    (*Savoring the sound.*) *Cleo.*
    Tomorrow, then.
    Same time?

TONY. Yes. Caesar and I
     will be in the Senate all morning.
     He'll be busy all afternoon,
     but I'll be free.

CLEO. What day is tomorrow?

TONY. The ides of March.

CLEO. Tony, I'll always remember today.

TONY. Yes, Cleo, and so will I!
     (*Dramatic.*) The feast of cunnilingus!

          (*They laugh.*)

CLEO. You *are* a naughty boy!

TONY. Tomorrow
     will be a feast day, too.
     The ides of March
     shall be called . . .
     (*Dramatic.*) the feast of fellati . . .

CLEO. (*Interrupting abruptly.*)
     I know! I know!
     You are a bad boy,
     and you are crude,
     just as people say.

TONY. (*Kneeling.*)
     In me tota ruens Venus!
     [The Goddess of Love

has descended on me
in full force!]

CLEO. (*Smiling.*)
Until tomorrow then . . . Tony.

TONY. (*Standing.*) Tomorrow . . . Cleo.

> (*He kisses her perfunctorily on the
> hand. They chuckle. He exits. She
> beams.*)

(*Fade-out.*)

Scene 3

44–41 BCE, narration.

EROS. (*Enters.*) The ides of March came,
but Tony and Cleo
did not keep their assignation.
Destiny had other plans.

Brutus and Cassius,
along with several other senators
desirous of keeping Rome
a republic based on liberty,
conspired to assassinate Julius Caesar
and did so.

Cleopatra, fearful for her life,
fled Rome for Alexandria. (*Pause.*)

Tony delivered an oration
after Caesar's assassination,
praising Caesar
and damning the assassins.
So moving was his speech
that it turned the Roman people
against Brutus and Cassius
and toward the dead Caesar's friends,
especially Tony, who,
now sole consul,
became the most powerful man
in Rome . . . until . . .
unexpectedly . . . Octavian,
Julius Caesar's nineteen-year-old nephew,
came to Rome
to hear the reading of Caesar's will.

Everyone was surprised to learn
that Caesar had adopted Octavian
as his son
and made him his principal heir.

And everyone was astonished
that Caesar had left
a legacy to the people of Rome—
to each Roman citizen
a small gift of money,
and to all of them collectively
some of his private gardens
to be used as public parks.

But in his will,
Caesar did not mention
the beloved Tony
at all.

TONY. (*Enters angrily.*)
Merda paedida!

EROS. [Stinking shit!]

TONY. The old man left me
ne sestertium quidem!

EROS. [Not even a silver coin!]

TONY. And to think he called me
his favorite and his darling boy!
Cinaede!

EROS. [Cocksucker!]

(TONY *exits.*)

Octavian took his adopted father's
family name of Caesar
and became Octavian Caesar.

Cicero, the great statesman
and orator, made it known
that Tony had been a male prostitute
in his youth;
and if a client happened
to fall in love with him,

Tony took advantage of him
by charging exorbitant prices.

So Cicero supported Octavian
and denounced Tony
as an opportunistic whore,
an enemy of the state,
and a civil-war maker,
and even compared him
to Helen of Troy,
the epitome of feminine beauty
and self-indulgence,
who led to Troy's destruction.

The disparaging comparison
had the desired effect.
The Senate turned on Tony
and made Octavian consul,
who took command
of the Roman army.

Tony fled to northern Italy,
where he was joined
by his old friend and ally
Marcus Aemilius Lepidus.
Octavian pursued
and defeated them there.

But Octavian,
knowing how crafty Tony was,
decided it was safer to have him
as a friend than an enemy.
So in 43 BCE,

Octavian reconciled
with Tony and Lepidus,
and they formed
a three-man dictatorship
called a triumvirate.

The following year, in 42 BCE,
Tony and Octavian
hunted down Caesar's assassins,
Brutus and Cassius, in Greece,
and Tony defeated them at Philippi.
Brutus and Cassius,
the last defenders of Roman liberty,
took the noble Roman exit.
They committed suicide.
Having dealt the deathblow
to the Roman Republic at Philippi,
Tony marched in triumph
throughout all Greece
and made Athens his home.

In 41 BCE
Tony summoned Cleopatra
to the city of Tarsus on the Cydnus
in Cilicia—
today called Turkey—
halfway between Athens and Alexandria.
That was the first time
they'd seen each other
since their initial meeting in Rome
three years earlier. (*Exits.*)

Scene 4

41 BCE, Tarsus on the Cydnus, Cilicia (Turkey), a riverboat.

(CHARMION *enters and lays a bed of pillows and cushions, then exits. CLEO enters, followed by* TONY. *They kiss long and passionately.*)

TONY. I never believed the rumor
    that you supported Brutus and Cassius
    against me at Philippi.
    How could a queen
    support Caesar's assassins
    when they despised the very words
    king and *queen*?
    Nonetheless, I summoned you here
    to let you defend yourself.
    To tell the truth,
    I was looking for any excuse to see you.
    And when I caught sight of you
    on the barge earlier today,
    a flame ignited in me
    that can never be extinguished.

    (*They kiss ardently.*)

    Because it was I
    who . . . invited . . . you to Tarsus,
    it was up to me
    to prepare a feast for you
    in the city,
    but you insisted

on giving a banquet for me
on this riverboat!

CLEO. No banquet compares
with the thought
of feasting on you!

TONY. I've been waiting three years
for this!

> (CLEO *pushes* TONY *down supine*
> *on the bed. She kneels over him*
> *and begins to shower him with*
> *kisses, starting with his mouth and*
> *moving toward his groin.*)

Behold! The naked truth!

CLEO. *Mentula tam magna est!*
[How big it is!]
The shaft is like silk,
the head is like velvet!
I want to kiss it!

TONY. Oh, do!

> (CLEO *performs oral sex. TONY*
> *moans. His cries of pleasure grow*
> *ever louder, ending in shouts fol-*
> *lowed by deep breathing. He sits*
> *up, takes her in his arms, and kisses*
> *her passionately.*)

CLEO. (*Smiling.*) Darling, are we even?

TONY. I don't ever want to be even!
    You've driven me
    completely out of my mind!
    I've been studying Greek philosophy,
    and the philosophers say,
    "The pleasures of the mind
    are superior to those of the body."

CLEO. The philosophers are fools!
    Just like the noblewomen who say,
    (*Mimicking pompously.*)
    "When I make love,
    I do so with dignity."
    No, not I! I'd never say anything
    as silly as that! (*Pause.*)
    Tony, I want to thank you.

TONY. Thank me? For what?

CLEO. Today, when my flagship
    dropped anchor in the harbor,
    I was told
    that you had made arrangements
    for this boat to carry me
    down the river to the city.
    But I was determined
    to show the world
    that I had come to Tarsus
    not because you ordered me to
    but because I wanted to.
    So I rigged and decorated

this riverboat in splendor,
showing not only
that I had come here freely
but also how happy I was
to be here,
never dreaming how happy
I'd really be!

TONY. Well, my dear,
you certainly made
a grand entrance!
I wrote a poem
in honor of the occasion.
Do you want to hear it?

CLEO. Yes, of course!

TONY. (*Standing and pantomiming
while reciting.*)

She sailed down the River Cydnus
from the harbor to the city of Tarsus
on a barge with a golden stern,
purple sails outspread before the wind,
silver oars beating time to the music
of pipes and lutes.

Cleopatra herself reclined
under a canopy spangled with gold,
adorned like sea-born Venus,
fanned by little boys,
each looking like Cupid,
standing on either side.

> Her fairest maids were dressed
> like sea nymphs or graces,
> two at the helm,
> others working the lines,
> each casting a look so sweet,
> it touched the hearts of all beholders
> and made them smile
> and hardly able to breathe.

CLEO. Oh, darling, *I* can hardly breathe!
   Your poem is enchanting!

TONY. Wait! There's more!

> Perfume diffused from the boat
> to the shores,
> where the dazzled crowds
> on either bank followed her,
> as others poured forth from the city
> to see the sight.

> The mobs in the marketplace
> drifted away
> until Marcus Antonius
> was left alone,
> sitting on the tribune's throne.

> Word went forth through the multitude
> that Venus was coming to dine
> with Bacchus
> to establish peace in the Middle East.

CLEO. *Peace in the Middle East!*
　　Oh, Tony!
　　Do you think that's possible?

TONY. Hush! My poem isn't over!

> When the barge landed,
> Antony invited Cleopatra
> to come ashore and dine with him,
> but she declined,
> preferring that he
> dine aboard with her.
> He complied willingly,
> showing his amicability.
>
> He found her preparations
> magnificent beyond description.
> But he was most amazed
> at the myriad of lights,
> a sight seldom equaled in beauty,
> and a spectacle the likes of which
> he'd never seen.
> And the banquet she'd prepared
> was worthy of the gods.

CLEO. Worthy of the gods!

TONY. *Now* it's over.
　　What do you think?

CLEO. Your poem is beautiful!
　　It exceeds my entrance into the city!

TONY. No, that is impossible!
   Nothing can compare with that!

    (CLEO *kisses him.*)

CLEO. But there *is* a line I don't understand.

TONY. Oh? Which?

CLEO. "Marcus Antonius was left alone,
   sitting on the tribune's throne."

TONY. (*Smiling.*) I couldn't very well
   let the whole world know
   I was the first one down to the dock!
   (*Suddenly serious.*)
   My dear, one moment of business!
   (*Confrontational.*) Tell me the truth!
   (*Staccato articulation.*) Did you finance
   Brutus and Cassius at Philippi?

CLEO. (*Standing, angrily.*)
   No, certainly not!
   Is that why you came?
   To ask for my financial support
   for some forthcoming military adventure
   of yours?

TONY. No.

    (*He presses her hand against his cheek.*)

I told you why I came—
to see you, to make love to you.

CLEO. Then why mention
Brutus and Cassius again—
and at such a moment?
That's like my asking you—
after we've made love—
whether you were loyal to Julius Caesar!

TONY. (*Obtusely.*) Darling, you asked me that
three years ago.

CLEO. As a matter of fact,
since then I've learned
it was *you* who started the rumor
that Caesar wanted to be king.

Exactly one month
before his assassination,
at the festival of the Lupercalia,
you raced up to Caesar's box
and placed a crown upon his head.
The crowd booed.
Caesar removed the crown
and handed it back to you.
The crowd cheered.
You did that three times,
and each time that you placed the crown
upon his head, the crowd booed.
And each time that he handed the crown
back to you, the crowd cheered.
Finally, you even fell prostrate

at his feet
as if he were a god!

It was those acts of yours
that set in motion
the wheels of his destruction.

No, you weren't a conspirator,
and you insist you were his friend,
but you got wind of the plot to kill him,
and yet you didn't warn him.

You say you loved him,
but didn't you want him dead?
And on his death,
didn't you expect to become
the most powerful man in Rome?

TONY. So, you're saying
I plotted Julius Caesar's death
and I successfully carried it out
without conspiring with anyone
and without actually killing him.

CLEO.   Darling, you're brilliant!
But your secret is safe with me.

TONY. Others know.

CLEO. Who?

TONY. That boy!—Octavian!—
Caesar's adopted son, for one!

Octavian became so afraid
I might one day
plot to have him assassinated, too,
that he made me his eternal ally. (*Pause.*)
Cleo, I didn't even know that boy existed
until he appeared
at the reading of Caesar's will.

CLEO. Can it be that *that boy*
is more cunning than Marcus Antonius?
But, darling, enough talk!

> (TONY *takes* CLEO *in his arms
> and kisses her passionately. She
> pushes him down supine on the bed
> and lies prone on top of him.*)

TONY. The touch of you
sets me on fire.

CLEO. (*Stroking his torso.*)
You are magnificent!

> (*They kiss again.* TONY *flips*
> CLEO *over on her back, lies prone
> on her, and begins to thrust.*)

> (*Fade-out.*)

Scene 5

A few weeks later, Rome, the palace of Octavian Caesar.

(*Trumpet fanfare.* OCTAVIAN *and* TONY *are conversing. The upstage wall holds a large map of the Mediterranean Sea and the surrounding territories.*)

TONY. Cleopatra had nothing to do
    with financing the battle of Philippi.

OCTAVIAN. How do you know?

TONY. She told me so.

OCTAVIAN. And you believe her?

TONY. Yes. She told me
    while we were making love.
    That's when people tell the truth.

OCTAVIAN. Did you ask her for money
    to finance any forthcoming
    military campaign?

TONY. No.

OCTAVIAN. Good!
    We don't need her money.
    Besides, you pay a whore.
    You don't take money from her.

TONY. She's not a whore, Caesar!

OCTAVIAN. Yes, I know.
 That's what my uncle—
 I mean my father . . . Julius—
 said, too.
 Anyway, Rome has the world
 and wealth in abundance,
 and I'm willing to share it all with you.

TONY. What about Lepidus?

OCTAVIAN. We'll give him a trifle,
 just enough to satisfy him.
 Here's what I had in mind.

 (*Pointing at the map as he indicates
 his division of the territories.*)

 With the Ionian Sea
 as the line of partition,
 I'll take the western provinces of Rome,
 including Italy, Gaul, and Hispania,
 and you'll take the eastern provinces,
 including Greece, Macedonia,
 and the Middle East.

TONY. And Lepidus?

OCTAVIAN. (*Pointing.*) We'll give him
 a segment of the north coast of Africa.

TONY. Africa—but without Egypt!

OCTAVIAN. *Without* Egypt?

TONY. Yes! Egypt belongs to Cleopatra.
     It is the kingdom of the Ptolemies.
     It is not a Roman province.

OCTAVIAN.   (*Hesitatingly.*) All right.
     Africa without Egypt. (*Sits down.*)

          (TONY *sits next to* OCTAVIAN.)

     That reminds me, Mark,
     you need a wife.
     I have just the woman for you.
     She's Roman, from a noble family,
     beautiful, intelligent—
     and the Romans adore her.

TONY. Who is she?

OCTAVIAN. My sister.

TONY. Your sister!

OCTAVIAN. Yes, Octavia.

TONY. Avia! I know her!
     I'd be honored
     to have her as my wife.

OCTAVIAN. Good!

TONY. But how do you know
    she'll have me?

OCTAVIAN. (*Placing a hand on* TONY*'s knee.*)
    Is there a woman in Rome
    who wouldn't want you for a husband?

TONY. (*Chuckling.*) Well, then,
    when's the wedding?

OCTAVIAN. (*Removing his hand.*)
    As soon as it can be arranged.

TONY. And when will you inform Lepidus
    of his share of the world?

OCTAVIAN. When the occasion
    is most auspicious—
    during your wedding reception.

TONY. (*Standing.*) Look,
    Lepidus is an old friend.
    I happen to know
    that all he really cares about
    is Sicily.

OCTAVIAN. (*Standing.*) Sicily is mine!

TONY. Well, don't be surprised if,
    (*Sarcastically.*) after you've *captured* it,
    he decides to take it from you.

OCTAVIAN. Let him try!
    Mark, everyone knows
    that Lepidus is
    the world's worst commander.
    Why, you're a better soldier
    when you're drunk
    than he is when he's sober!

    (*They laugh,* TONY *reservedly.*)

    Besides, Lepidus loves Jupiter
    more than Sicily.
    So I'd consecrate him—
    I'd confirm him as *pontifex maximus*,
    chief priest of Rome,
    and give him a palace on Palatine Hill.
    He'd like that.

    Mark, I know that Lepidus
    is your friend.
    He's a nice fellow,
    but frankly
    he's not very good at politics
    and not good at all at intrigue—
    and he hates confrontation—
    so I seriously doubt
    he's going to go to war
    against me over Sicily.
    Besides, he's richer than Midas.
    So commander in chief
    of the Roman religion . . .
    with a beautiful palace . . .
    in the very best residential neighborhood

in Rome . . .
is the very thing!
All he really wants from life
is to wallow in luxury.
Surely you can understand that.

TONY. I have higher aspirations.
I am going to marry Caesar's sister.
We're going to make our home in Greece,
where I intend to become
another famous Greek philosopher!

> (*They laugh,* OCTAVIAN *sardonically.*)

> (*Fade-out.*)

Scene 6

40 BCE, Rome, the palace of Octavian Caesar; Athens, Tony's mansion.

EROS. (*Enters.*) And so, several months later, in 40 BCE,

> (OCTAVIAN, AVIA, *and* TONY *enter and pantomime. They begin with* OCTAVIAN*'s giving* AVIA *to* TONY.)

Tony married Avia,
Caesar's favorite sister,

in a splendid wedding in Rome.
Everyone was sure
his beautiful new wife

> (TONY *and* AVIA *kiss and caress
> each other ardently.*)

would make him forget Cleopatra.
Marcus Aemilius Lepidus
was among the wedding guests
and was delighted to receive—
in addition to a slice of wedding cake—
a slice of Africa.

The newlyweds began married life
in Tony's home in Athens.
At first he enjoyed his new wife,

> (TONY *and* AVIA *continue to
> embrace.*)

but soon his thoughts turned again
to Cleopatra,

> (CLEO *enters and strokes* TONY*'s
> shoulders and arms while* TONY *is
> caressing* AVIA. AVIA *slowly steps
> back and disengages, sensing
> something is the matter.*)

and he couldn't get her out of his mind.

> (*Fade-out.*)

Scene 7

Later that year, Athens, Tony's mansion.

EROS.   But then,
    in the same year, 40 BCE,
    the barbarian empire of Parthia
    invaded the Roman province of Syria.
    Today, what was the Parthian Empire
    includes the modern nations
    Iraq, Iran, Afghanistan, and Pakistan.
    Parthia constantly made border wars
    against its neighbors
    and kept the Middle East in turmoil.
    It was a thorn in Rome's side.
    Tony summoned his friend
    General Ventidius
    to come to Athens
    to discuss the solution
    to Parthian aggression
    against Rome.

> (VENTIDIUS *enters in full military
> armor. He removes his helmet and
> hands it to* EROS, *who exits.*)

VENTIDIUS. (*To the audience.*)
    My name is Publius Ventidius Bassus.
    People call me simply Ventidius.
    I served as an officer in Gaul—
    today you call it France—
    under Julius Caesar along with Tony,
    whom you call Marcus Antonius.

Tony and I are old friends,
and we were Julius Caesar's favorite officers.
Most of you have never heard of me.
My parents were freed slaves.
The army allowed me to become
a self-made man,
but it was my friendship
with Tony that gave me the chance
to show off my military skills.
So I owe him a great deal.

Tony outshone me in breeding,
in looks, and in personality.
But, in fact, I was Caesar's
most valuable soldier.
If you doubt it, ask Tony.

Now, Tony could have been
the most valuable soldier.
Julius Caesar considered him
the finest officer
who'd ever served under him—
his military skill, his courage,
his authoritative manner,
and his popularity with the men.
He liked to walk through the campsites,
making himself visible to the soldiers,
chatting and joking with them.
And when they were eating,
he'd sit down and join them.
That delighted them,
and they adored him.

But as much as his men loved him,
and he them,
other things had a greater hold on him—
wine and women,
particularly other men's wives,
but he did not disdain camp followers.
He had no self-control.
All those nights of revelry!
All those days sleeping off hangovers!
And he always seemed
to be looking elsewhere.
If a woman appeared, off they'd go,
even at the height of battle.

And Julius Caesar let him get away with it
because Caesar liked him—
liked him a lot.

Tony is a sex addict.
He'd frequently say to me,

    (TONY *enters.*)

"Ventidi,
quid quod mihi vita carior
est ipsa mentula."

TONY. [Ventidius,
my cock's more dear to me
than life itself.]

VENTIDIUS. Sometimes he'd say,
  "Futuere melior est quam pugnare."

TONY. [It's better to fuck
  than to fight.]

VENTIDIUS.   Believe me,
  he lived by that motto.
  He was ruled by the God of Love.
  As for me, I am lucky.
  My mistress is always
  at my side, ready to serve me.
  Her name is Dextra,
  which means right hand.
  You see,
  I am . . . a *masturbator*.
  That's a Latin word,
  and I hope you forgive me
  for not knowing how to say it
  in English.
  Unlike me, Tony was satisfied
  only with the real thing—*cunni*.
  I know I don't have to translate that!
  He used to say,
  "Quam futuis, vocas amicam."

TONY. [The girl you fuck
  is the one you call girlfriend.]

VENTIDIUS.   Now, if a week went by
  without a woman,
  any warm body would do.
  Then he'd say . . .

TONY. (*Smiling.*) Ventidius,
the only difference
between a woman and a man
is that a woman has one more hole.
(*Grinning broadly and winking.*)

> (*Saluting* VENTIDIUS.)

Salve, Ventidi!

VENTIDIUS. (*Returning the salute.*)

Salve, Antoni!

> (*They clasp forearms in the Roman
> style of greeting.*)

TONY. I sent for you
because, as you know,
the Parthians have invaded Syria.
I want you
to lead an expedition
to drive the Parthians out.

VENTIDIUS. My lord, I'd be honored!

TONY. Good! How many legions
do you think you'll need?

VENTIDIUS. Ten should do it.

TONY. To be on the safe side,
    we'll gather twenty, all well trained.
    And I'll ask Octavian Caesar
    to send his best men. (*Pause.*)
    Are you sure twenty legions
    will be enough?

VENTIDIUS. More than enough.

TONY. You're sure you don't want
    to invade the Parthian Empire,
    conquer it,
    and make it a Roman province?

VENTIDIUS. No, that would be
    overextending ourselves.
    A limited war
    to drive the Parthians from Syria
    is a reasonable goal.
    Such a war can be won.

TONY. Julius Caesar wanted to invade
    and conquer Parthia
    and make it a Roman province.

VENTIDIUS. Julius Caesar
    did not always exhibit good judgment—
    and he was murdered
    just before he got to try that.

TONY. How long do you think it'll take—
    I mean, to drive the Parthians from Syria?

VENTIDIUS. That's hard to say.
    At least two years, maybe three.
    That's why trying to do more
    would not be productive.
    Our losses would vastly exceed our gains.
    Besides, the Parthian Empire is invincible.
    The terrain is barren and hostile.
    Food and water are not plentiful.
    The people are savage and tribal.
    When they're not fighting foreigners,
    they're fighting one another.
    And even if we could conquer them,
    what then?
    They'd never accept a Roman peace.
    They don't know the meaning of peace.
    And they'd never abide by Roman law.
    They're a law unto themselves.
    And their values are not Roman values.
    They fight as if they loved death
    more than life.
    So there's no way to invade Parthia
    and conquer it.
    The war would go on forever.
    No. I'll drive the Parthians from Syria,
    and then we'll call it quits.

(Fade-out.)

Scene 8

37 BCE, Athens, Tony's mansion.

EROS. (*Enters.*) Ventidius entered Syria.
    After three major battles
    over three years,
    and after killing
    the top three enemy generals,
    he drove the Parthians from Syria.
    Ventidius returned to Athens
    to give a report to Tony.

> (EROS *exits*. TONY *and* VEN-
> TIDIUS *enter from opposite sides
> and clasp forearms.*)

VENTIDIUS. Commander,
    Syria is once again Roman!

TONY. So I've heard!
    Well done, Ventidius!

VENTIDIUS. The peace treaty
    remains to be signed,
    and I think you should sign it.

TONY. Then Rome will give me the glory
    for the victory that *you* have won.

VENTIDIUS. What does it matter
    who gets the glory?
    The important thing is we've won.

TONY. That's just like you, Ventidius.
   It was the same
   under Julius Caesar in Gaul.
   You'd win the battle,
   but you'd report to Caesar
   that you couldn't have done it
   without me,
   even when I'd been—
   shall we say?—
   elsewhere.
   What made you cover for me?

VENTIDIUS. Caesar liked hearing
   only good reports about you,
   and it's important
   to keep the commander happy.
   His happiness keeps up morale.
   And you score more victories
   when morale is high.

TONY. Well, I'm not taking any glory
   here.
   No one has ever before
   been victorious over the Parthians.
   You're the first!
   So you can count on
   a well-deserved triumph
   in Rome.

VENTIDIUS. Thank you, Commander.
   And now, (*Saluting*.) *Antoni, vale!*

TONY. (*Saluting.*) *Ave atque vale!*

>   (VENTIDIUS *exits.* AVIA *enters
>   and kisses* TONY.)

AVIA. Good news, I hear!
    You've driven the Parthians
    from Syria!

TONY. Ventidius did it, not I.
    The victory is all his.
    It's funny
    how the people who love me
    have a need to make me out a winner.
    Julius Caesar did that,
    and now you do, too.

AVIA. Well, you did win.
    You are the commander in chief
    of the Middle East.
    And it was you
    who appointed Ventidius.

TONY. But I didn't go into the field.
    The whole time
    Ventidius was fighting in Syria,
    I was living the good life here in Greece.
    Now he wants me to go to Syria
    to sign the peace treaty.
    Well, I'll go and I'll sign it,
    but I'm sending him back to Rome
    to march in a triumphal parade.
    The glory is all his.

AVIA. That's very generous of you.
    But you're famous for that.
    You're generous to a fault.

TONY. (*Contemplating.*) What if,
    instead of signing a peace treaty,
    I invaded the Parthian Empire,
    conquered it,
    and made it a Roman province?
    Julius Caesar wanted to do that,
    but he never got the chance.
    If I conquered Parthia,
    I would have civilized a savage nation
    that gives Rome nothing but trouble
    and honorably won some glory for myself.

AVIA. You want to outdo Julius Caesar?
    Have you discussed this
    with Ventidius?

TONY. He doesn't like the idea.
    He says it's impossible to conquer Parthia,
    and I'd be devastated in trying.

AVIA. Ventidius is a wise man.

TONY. But I want to win a war
    all by myself!
    My enemies say my victories
    have been achieved
    by my generals, not me!
    That's not how I want
    posterity to remember me!

AVIA. What do you care
     what your enemies say?
     Marcus Antonius,
     posterity will remember you
     as a great soldier and a great leader.
     The campaign
     to drive the Parthians from Syria
     is over.
     You won it as much as Ventidius.
     And so you should be planning
     a victory celebration,
     not engaging in self-deprecation!

TONY. No! This is not the time
     for celebration.
     I will invade Parthia
     and conquer it
     and make it a Roman province!
     And *then* we can celebrate!

               (*Fade-out.*)

               Scene 9

*December 36 BCE, somewhere in the Parthian Em-
pire, the Roman campsite.*

EROS. (*Enters.*) Well,
     Tony invaded the Parthian Empire,
     but he did not conquer it.
     The Parthian campaign

was an unmitigated disaster.
When Tony won,
the gains were trivial;
when he was defeated,
the losses were great.
And here we are, still in Parthia—
and this winter has been brutal.

TONY. (*Entering, to the audience.*)
I didn't conquer Parthia.
The terrain was harsher
than I'd anticipated,
the inhabitants more savage,
but worst of all,
I met up with three unexpected enemies
far fiercer than the Parthians—
Winter, Starvation, and Disease.
Thousands of troops
have lost their lives in battle,
and thousands more
have been carried back to camp
sick or wounded,
and of those, almost half died.

EROS. But in spite of that,
Tony's men love him,
especially because he goes
from tent to tent
giving comfort to the wounded and dying.

(CORNELIUS, *his head in bloody
bandages, is carried in on a
stretcher and set down.*)

TONY. (*Kneeling at* CORNELIUS*'s side.*)
    How are you doing, Soldier?

CORNELIUS. (*Clasping* TONY*'s arm.*)
    As long as you're well, General,
    I'm well, too.

TONY. Do you feel safe?

CORNELIUS. As long as you're unharmed,
    I'm safe, Commander.

TONY. (*Trying to make a joke.*)
    How's the food, Soldier?

CORNELIUS. We've been living mostly
    on roots, bark, rodents, pebbles,
    and even dirt.

> (CORNELIUS *begins to retch.*
> EROS *removes and unplugs his
> own canteen.* TONY *offers it to*
> CORNELIUS.)

TONY. Take a sip of water, Soldier.

CORNELIUS. (*Sips.*) I feel better now.
    Thank you, General.
    You don't have to worry about me.
    Just take care of yourself.

TONY. What's your name, Soldier?

CORNELIUS. Cornelius, General.

TONY. (*Taking* CORNELIUS *'s hand in his own.*)
And mine is Marcus Antonius.

CORNELIUS. I know that, General.
The whole world knows that!

TONY. Cornelius, you're a brave man.
And I want to thank you
for all you've done for Rome.

CORNELIUS. General,
I've not done it for Rome.
I've done it for you.
Your caring about me
means more to me than my life.
Vale, Commander.

TONY. Not *vale*!
Cornelius, I'll come by tomorrow
and see how you're doing.

CORNELIUS. Thank you, General.

(*Fade-out.*)

(TONY *and* EROS *enter shivering.*)

TONY. There's nothing to be gained
by staying here any longer.
Ventidius was right.

We should never have come.
We've accomplished nothing
except bring disaster on ourselves.
It's all my doing.
Eros, what do you think
we should do now?

EROS. My lord,
I think we should go home.
There's no point in staying
when there's no hope of winning,
and this winter is never ending!
We've already lost
twenty thousand infantry
and four thousand cavalry,
more than half by disease.

TONY. Should we surrender?

EROS. (*Shaking his head.*)
Romans do not surrender.
We should just leave.
Win or lose,
the people back home will never know.
Tell them we've won,
and then, my lord, we've won!

TONY. But we *have* won, Eros,
we *have*, don't you see?
For if we flee, we're victorious
because we've escaped with our lives!

(EROS *looks at* TONY *quizzically.*)

By the way, how's Cornelius doing—
the soldier I visited last night?

EROS. Cornelius died at dawn, my lord.

(*Fade-out.*)

Scene 10

January 35 BCE, White Village Harbor, Syria, Tony's ship.

EROS. A month later.
   White Village Harbor, Syria,
   aboard Tony's ship at anchor.
   Cleo, fearful that Tony
   would return to his wife in Athens,
   and determined that he return
   to Alexandria with her,
   sailed from Egypt
   to his port of embarkation in Syria.

TONY. (*Drunk. Reading a letter.*)
   "Darling Tony,
   Be sure to wait for me at White Village Harbor.
   Don't leave before I get there.
   I'll die if I don't see you.
   Your Cleo."
   This letter came a month ago.
   And still she's not here.
   What could be causing the delay?

EROS. Something unforeseen
   has happened,
   but there's no point in thinking
   it's necessarily bad.

> (TONY *shows drunken affection toward* EROS.)

TONY. It's been so long
   since I've had a lay.
   You better watch out, Eros!

EROS. Well, I sure hope she comes soon!

TONY. (*Drinking.*) It sounds as if
   you've been getting some, Eros.
   Where have you been getting it?
   A city girl or a country girl?
   What's the difference? Right?
   (*Suddenly agitated.*) Where is Cleo?
   Why hasn't she come?
   Where has *she* been getting it
   this long time away from me?

EROS. My lord,
   you're the only one she loves.
   You know that.
   Maybe her ship was detained
   in Alexandria—
   to repair planking
   or patch sails.
   Or maybe a storm delayed them.

(TONY *paces anxiously and con-*
tinues to drink. EROS, looking at
the harbor, suddenly becomes
excited.)

My Lord, look there! A boat!
Yes, a ship! And it's Egyptian!

(EROS *hurriedly adjusts* TONY*'s*
tunic and smooths his hair. TONY
blows breath toward EROS*'s nose.*
EROS *gestures as if to say "good*
enough.")

CLEO. (*Enters with excitement.*)
Sweetheart, I'm so happy to see you!

(TONY *and* CLEO *embrace and*
kiss passionately. EROS *exits.*)

I'm sorry I was so delayed.
We encountered a severe storm
off the coast of Judea.

TONY. Judea!
So the Jews are even responsible
for bad weather!

(*They again embrace and kiss*
passionately.)

CLEO. You've been drinking!

TONY. I had to do something
    to distract myself
    from worrying about you.

        (*They kiss again.*)

    By Jove, you look wonderful!

CLEO. And so do you!
    Tony, I had to see you
    the moment the war was over.
    (*Hesitantly.*) It is over, isn't it?

TONY. Yes, it's over.

CLEO. Well, who won?

TONY. They did.
    But what's the difference?
    I'm alive,
    and we're together again!

CLEO. I agree!

        (*They kiss again.*)

    Oh, darling, let's return to Alexandria!

TONY. (*Somber.*) I can't!
    I have to go home
    to give a full report
    of my . . . misadventure

in Parthia.
If I go to Alexandria instead,
Caesar
and the Senate and the People of Rome
. . . and Avia . . .
will turn against me.
They'll accuse me of insolence
and contempt for my native land.

CLEO. But Greece isn't your native land!

TONY. Greece is a Roman province,
and my wife and home are in Athens.

CLEO. But there's no one
in Athens or Rome
who cares about you
like I do.

TONY. They all care about me—
Athens, Rome, Caesar . . . Avia.
And if I don't return to them
because I choose to stay with you,
I'm afraid there will be civil war—
war over a woman.

CLEO. Rome wouldn't go to war
over me!

TONY. You're not the woman
I had in mind.

CLEO. Well, whom are you talking about?

TONY. Me! Cicero said that I was a woman,
　　　that I came between men like a woman,
　　　that I enjoyed having men fight over me
　　　like a woman,
　　　and that I was as responsible
　　　for civil war in Rome
　　　as Helen was for the Trojan War!

CLEO. Well, I'll be happy to tell anyone
　　　you're not a woman!

TONY. When Cicero wasn't calling me
　　　a destructive whore,
　　　he was calling me
　　　the stupidest man alive.

CLEO. *Di boni!* [Good gods!]

TONY. And he'd say it over and over
　　　in many different ways,
　　　and his words echoed
　　　throughout the world:

　　　　　(*Actors delivering the Latin appear,
　　　　　say their line, then disappear.*)

VENTIDIUS. *"Hominum stultissime!"*

TONY. ["Dumbest of men!"] (*Pause.*)

AVIA. *"Homo amentissime!"*

TONY. ["Most mindless man!"] (*Pause.*)

OCTAVIAN. *"Incredibilem stupiditatem
    hominis cognoscite!"*

TONY. ["Consider the incredible stupidity
    of the man!"] (*Pause.*)

EROS. *"Nec enim est ab homine
    numquam sobrio
    postulanda prudentia."*

TONY. ["You can't expect intelligence
    from a man who's never sober."]

    Well, Cicero certainly knew
    what he was talking about!
    So I had to kill him.
    What choice did I have?

CLEO. Tony, forget Cicero!
    Think about me!
    We haven't seen each other
    for so long!
    I almost died during that time.

TONY. *Died?* From what?

CLEO. From not seeing you!
    Oh, darling, you are my world!
    Without you . . .
    (*In dire anguish.*)
    what will become of me?

Have you become so hardhearted
and unfeeling?
Do you intend to destroy me,
who is devoted to you and you alone?

Octavia married you
as a matter of Roman policy
and to protect her brother from you.
And she enjoys
the good name of "wife."
But I, Cleopatra, Queen of Egypt,
am called Antony's whore and mistress.
I've stained the glory of my royal house
and lost all honor
because of you.

But what is that
as long as I can see you,
(*Savoring each phrase.*)
touch you, kiss you, talk with you,
live with you, enjoy you?
If you leave me now,
I cannot survive.
Darling, return to Alexandria
with me!
Oh, Tony, *da mi basia mille!*
Deinde centum!
[Give me a thousand kisses!
Then a hundred more!]
Come to me, my soldier,
come to my arms!
You've been far too long
from my embrace.

(*He stares at her for a long moment. Then he takes her in his arms. They kiss passionately.*)

Oh, my life! My soul! My all!

TONY. Did I ever tell you
that I love you?

CLEO. No, never. Tell me!

TONY. (*With great tenderness.*)
I love you. I adore you.
I never get my fill of you!
Who needs the world
as long as I have you?
Who needs anything
as long as I have you?

(*Commanding.*) Eros!
Make all the necessary preparations!
We sail for Alexandria!

(*Fade-out.*)

INTERMISSION

INTERLUDE

A dance similar to the one that began Act I but ominous as well as sensuous.

(Fade-out.)

ACT II

Scene 1

35 BCE, Alexandria, the royal bedroom.

(TONY *and* CLEO *are in bed giggling and play-fully enjoying each other. After a moment,* EROS *enters, and* TONY *and* CLEO *pantomime* EROS*'s speech.*)

EROS. (*Enters.*) It is now 35 BCE.
   The place is Alexandria.

   After Tony returned
   to Alexandria with Cleo
   following the Parthian disaster,
   there was nothing but *flagrans amor*
   [burning love].
   They were inseparable,
   and they enjoyed
   only each other's company.

She constantly contributed
some fresh delight
and irresistible charm
to stimulate and satisfy him.
Their conversation was endless
and covered all subjects,
and she taught him things
he'd never known before.
This went on day after day,
night after night.

>   (TONY *and* CLEO *leave the bed,
>   put on robes, and continue to pan-
>   tomime.*)

She played dice with him,
drank with him,
went hunting and fishing with him,
and joined him in practicing sword play
or javelin throwing;
and afterward
they would bathe together. (*Exits.*)

CLEO. Tony, are you really dangerous
and ruthless?

TONY. Yes. And I kill all my enemies!

CLEO. I'm glad I'm your friend.

TONY. (*Grinning.*) Me, too.

CLEO. Did you kill Cicero brutally,
    as people say?

TONY. Most brutally.

> (*Demonstrating by gently caressing*
> CLEO*'s neck and hands* while
> *speaking in dead earnest.*)

I ordered him decapitated
and his hands cut off.
And when the assassins
delivered those parts to me,
I had them nailed up in the Forum
for everyone to see.

CLEO. How grisly!

TONY. Did you know that Cicero
    was the prosecuting attorney
    who brought about
    my stepfather's death?

CLEO. Is that why you hated him so?

TONY. No. He was guilty,
    just as Cicero said.

CLEO. Did you hate him
    because he called you
    the true assassin of Julius Caesar?

TONY. No. I guess that was true, too.
　　None of those things
　　would have made me kill Cicero,
　　not even when he called me a whore.
　　It was when he called me
　　"dumbest of men!"

CLEO. Forget it! You're not dumb!

TONY. Did you know, Cleo,
　　that I'm personally responsible
　　for the death
　　of the three most influential men
　　who wanted liberty for Rome—
　　Cicero, Brutus, and Cassius.

CLEO. And Julius Caesar?

TONY. Well, there's no doubt
　　he loved the Roman people;
　　but he was a dictator
　　and loved absolute power, too,
　　so I was never really sure—
　　I don't think anyone else was, either—
　　whether he was a tyrant
　　or a lover of liberty.

CLEO. And you? Which are you?

TONY. Oh, I'm a tyrant.
　　Give me tyranny or give me death!
　　Actually, I harbor the two extremes—
　　tyranny and liberty—

simultaneously,
and I've committed monstrous crimes
for the sake of them both.

CLEO. That's enough politics for today!

TONY. (*Gazing at her eagerly.*)
My sight feasts as much as my touch.

(*He kisses her.*)

Your mouth and lips are delicious.

CLEO. (*Stroking the back of his neck.*)
Did you know that when I catch
a glimpse of the back of your neck,
it drives me insane?

TONY. (*Caressing each body part
as he mentions it.*)
The sight of your breasts and legs
does the same to me,
as does your smooth, round belly
and your dainty little feet.
But that charming cleft
where your two thighs meet
is dearest of all to me.
I want to drown in the flowing juices
and smother in the silky hair.

(*He sweeps her up and places her
on the bed, then crawls on top of
her.*)

CLEO. *Di boni!* [Good gods!]
    Don't drown or smother!
    That would defeat the purpose!

TONY. Oh, I want to fill it with wine
    and drink to the dregs!

CLEO. No, you silly!
    You've already had
    too much to drink!

    (*They engage, and he begins to thrust.*)

TONY. Oh, I can't stand it!
    Do you enjoy this as much as I do?

CLEO.   How can we ever know?

    (*Thrusting continues, but then he
    abruptly freezes.*)

TONY. Don't move!
    Don't even breathe!

    (*Momentary inactivity and silence.*)

    Now! Oh, kiss me now! Hard!

    (*They kiss. He resumes thrusting but
    more rapidly. Moans and cries of
    pleasure.*)

    (*Fade-out.*)

Scene 2

A year later, Athens, Tony's mansion.

(AVIA *and* TONY, *who is a figment of Avia's imagination, are standing back-to-back.*)

EROS. (*Appears.*) A year later.
    Avia is all alone in Tony's home in Athens.
    (*Disappears.*)

        (TONY *remains immobile* as AVIA
        walks around to face him.)

AVIA. (*Distraught.*) Antony,
    do you intend to ignore me forever
    and let me die of loneliness
    in a foreign land,
    I, who depend on you so?

        (*She caresses his face.*)

    Oh, Antony, how I need you!
    And your children need you, too—
    beautiful children . . . and bright.
    But what do you care
    about your children?
    I hear that Cleopatra
    has also given you some,
    and you ignore hers
    as much as mine. (*Pause.*)

Oh, I know that you married me
out of convenience,
to gain half the Roman world,
and that I'm your wife in name only.
I accept the heartache of the wife
whose husband loves another woman.
What makes my suffering unbearable
is that I still love you.

(*She kisses him ardently.*)

(*Happily, expectantly.*) I've prepared
a great homecoming in your honor.
Throughout Greece
games are being played.
And in the theaters, revivals continue
of the comedies by Aristophanes
that you loved so much.

(*She tenderly strokes his face.*)

(*Anguished.*) Antony,
you are returning home to me,
aren't you?

EROS. (*Enters.*) My lady, I have a message
from your husband.

AVIA. Oh!

EROS. (*Reading.*) "From Marcus Antonius,
Commander of the Roman provinces
of the East,

To Avia, my dear wife in Athens.
Greetings!
I am well,
and the Parthian campaign is long over.

> (CLEO, *another figment of Avia's
> imagination, enters and embraces*
> TONY.)

"But I won't be returning
to Athens as soon as I had wished.
A situation has arisen in Egypt
that requires my undivided attention.

> (TONY *and* CLEO *kiss ardently,
> then exit arm in arm.*)

"More later.
Your devoted husband,
Marcus Antonius."

AVIA. (*Bitterly.*) "My *dear* wife . . .
Your *devoted* husband."
(*Bursting into tears.*)

*Antoni, irascor tibi,
et sic meos amores?*
[Antony, I'm mad for you,
and this is how you treat my love?]

(*To* EROS, *angrily.*)
That other woman!
What can he possibly see in her

now that she's not twenty anymore?
I hear it takes Egyptian makeup
to cover the wrinkles on her brow,
and black dye to color the gray hairs.
But he still can't take his eyes off her,
can't get enough of her.

(*Composed.*) Well,
I've got to face reality,
the sooner the better.
What is there for me in Athens?
(*Resolutely.*) I shall return to Rome,
where I have my brother
and a home
more comfortable than this
and with all the conveniences
I'm used to.
I'll have my friends again
and be among Romans—
people who speak Latin—
and I'll have cooks
who prepare Roman meals
and my favorite dishes.

(*To* EROS.) Eros,
make all the necessary preparations.
I wish to return to Rome at once!

EROS. Yes, my lady.

(*Fade-out.*)

Scene 3

32 BCE, Rome, the palace of Octavian Caesar.

EROS. Two years later, 32 BCE.
    Rome. The palace of Octavian Caesar. (*Exits.*)

      (*Trumpet fanfare.*)

AVIA. (*Lying on the floor, weeping.   Then crying
    out in despair.*)
    Octavian! Brother!

      (OCTAVIAN *rushes in.*)

    Instead of coming home to me
    from Parthia,
    Antony went to Egypt.
    That was over three years ago,
    and he's still in Egypt!
    He is chained and bound
    to that woman!

      (OCTAVIAN *helps* AVIA *to her
      feet.*)

OCTAVIAN. He likes the chains
    that bind him.
    She controls him completely,
    has total power over him.
    But mark my words!
    She's going to humiliate him

and then she's going to destroy him.
That's the ultimate power play.

AVIA. He is beyond humiliation!

OCTAVIAN. No man
is beyond humiliation.
Believe me,
she will find a way.

AVIA. Perhaps he wants
to be destroyed.
Isn't there anything you can do
to prevent it?

OCTAVIAN. (*Sardonically.*)
We can always go to war.

AVIA. No. You can't go to war
over Antony's treatment of me.
It would be a terrible thing
if people said
that the two most powerful men
in the world,
Marcus Antonius and Octavian Caesar,
plunged the Romans into civil war—
Antony out of passion for Cleopatra
and Caesar out of resentment
for the shabby treatment of his sister.

OCTAVIAN. Avia, the Roman people
don't like men
who treat noblewomen badly.

And they don't like Romans
who become slaves
to foreign women.
We have reports that in Alexandria,
during state dinners
with Cleopatra at his side,
he massages and kisses her feet!

AVIA. Well, we know he can act like a fool,
but you can't go to war over that.

OCTAVIAN. We have other reports
that during Roman affairs of state,
from which Cleopatra
has been excluded,
she sends him love notes,
which he proceeds to read aloud,
disrupting the meeting
and embarrassing everyone in attendance.
Sometimes,
without even excusing himself,
he abruptly dashes forth
from such meetings
to go running after her.

AVIA. They act like spoiled children
who only want to gain attention.
But behavior unbecoming
a Roman head of state
is not grounds for war,
particularly when you've accepted
such behavior from him
for a long time.

OCTAVIAN. You're right, of course.
      He loved to go on picnics
      but insisted on being served—
      in the country, in a field, on the grass!—
      in bowls of gold
      and in cups of exquisite glass!
      And many times
      he'd come to the Roman Forum
      after a night of drinking
      and puke all over his toga!
      But you can't go to war over that.
      We need him to do
      something egregious—
      to make an attack,
      real or perceived, on Rome.

EROS. (*Entering and saluting.*)
      Hail, Caesar! Hail, Octavia!
      I bring you news.

OCTAVIAN. Speak!

EROS. (*Reading aloud.*)
      "From Marcus Antonius,
      Commander of the Roman provinces
      of the East.
      To Octavia, my wife.
      I hereby order you
      to leave my house in Rome."

AVIA. (*Shrieking.*) What did I tell you!

OCTAVIAN. To drive a wife from home
    is to banish her from bed.
    To banish her from bed
    is divorce.

AVIA. Divorce me? To marry her?

OCTAVIAN. No! No Roman
    would marry
    (*Contemptuously.*) an Egyptian!
    She's his mistress.
    She'll never get a title higher than that.

AVIA. Mistress of Marcus Antonius!
    Not a bad title!
    Many women would like to have it.
    (*In anguish.*) I would! (*Sobbing.*)

OCTAVIAN. Avia, control yourself!

AVIA. Eros, does he intend
    to marry her?

EROS. He never mentioned that,
    my lady.
    But there's more in his letter.

AVIA. I can't bear to hear more!

OCTAVIAN. (*To* EROS.) Keep reading!

EROS. "Marcus Antonius
    hereby informs Caesar

>that he has made gifts to Cleopatra,
>Queen of Egypt."

OCTAVIAN. Gifts? What kind of gifts?
Perfume from Arabia?
Jewelry? A gold necklace, perhaps?

EROS. Gifts far more substantial!

OCTAVIAN. A villa in the country?
A summer home by the sea?

EROS. Far more substantial!

>(TONY *appears.   When* TONY
>*speaks,* EROS *freezes.   When* EROS
>or others *speak,* TONY *freezes.*)

OCTAVIAN. Keep reading!

EROS. "Marcus Antonius
declares to Caesar
and the whole world:" (*Freezes.*)

TONY. I have given Cleopatra,
Queen of Egypt,
all the eastern provinces of Rome,
including Arabia, Phoenicia, Judea,
Cyprus, Syria, Cilicia,
and, if I ever conquer it, Parthia. (*Freezes.*)

OCTAVIAN. (*Sardonically.*) *Parthia*, too,
if he ever conquers it!

(*Raging*.) Marcus Antonius is a fool
and the stupidest man alive!
Everything Cicero said of him is true!
Marcus Antonius was assigned
the eastern provinces
to rule on behalf of Rome.
They belong to Rome eternally!
He has no authority to give them away.
Does he think he can trade
kingdoms for kisses?
Giving away all those taxes!
All that grain! All those slaves!
All that income!
The Roman economy will be ruined!

AVIA. (*Bitterly*.) He's always been generous.

EROS. (*Animated*.) Marcus Antonius
   calls his gifts . . . (*Freezes*.)

TONY. (*Animated, dramatic*.)
   the "Donations of Alexandria." (*Freezes*.)

OCTAVIAN. *Donations!*
   Positively philanthropic!
   Has she accepted them?

EROS. (*Animated*.) She has!
   And she has already assumed absolute rule
   over all of them. (*Pause*.)
   Marcus Antonius says, (*Freezes*.)

TONY. (*Animated.*) The greatness of Rome
       lies more in giving away kingdoms
       than in taking them. (*Freezes.*)

OCTAVIAN. I see. So,
       according to (*Contemptuously.*) *him*,
       it is better to give than to receive!
       I suppose he wants me to carve that slogan
       in gigantic letters over the Senate!
       What else does our *Greek philosopher*
       have to say?

TONY. (*Animated.*) The way
       to carry noble blood
       throughout the world
       is not by conquest
       but by fathering in every place
       a new line of kings. (*Freezes.*)

OCTAVIAN. Oh! So,
       according to him,
       Rome's motto should be
       Make Love, Not War.

AVIA. That's always been his motto!

EROS. Then he's way ahead of his time!

OCTAVIAN. (*Menacing.*) Eros,
       cease from your master's audacity!
       Another comment like that,
       and I shall be forced to punish you, too!

EROS. I beg Caesar's pardon.

AVIA. Brother,
    don't blame the messenger!

EROS. Marcus Antonius writes
    one last thing. (*Freezes.*)

OCTAVIAN. Yes?

TONY. (*Animated.*) In my will,
    I have requested
    that if I should happen
    to die in Rome,
    I want a full state funeral in the Forum.
    But afterward I want my remains
    shipped to Cleopatra
    for burial in Alexandria. (*Disappears.*)

OCTAVIAN. (*Angrily.*) Unlimited audacity!
    Have you finished, Eros?

EROS. Yes, my lord.

OCTAVIAN. Tomorrow, Eros,
    you shall read this letter
    in the Senate.
    Et Senatus Populusque Romanus
    [And the Senate and the People of Rome]
    will strip (*Contemptuously.*) Marcus Antonius
    of all authority and power
    and make his so-called donations
    null and void. And then

Senatus Populusque Romanus
[the Senate and the People of Rome]
shall declare war on Cleopatra
because, in accepting these . . . *donations* . . .
she has illegally assumed control
of half the Roman world!

(*Fade-out.*)

Scene 4

A few weeks later, Alexandria, the royal bedroom.

(TONY *and* CLEO *are in bed rolling about but hidden by the sheets.*)

TONY. (*Suddenly anxious, pulling down the sheet
    from his upper body, sitting up, and inspecting
    and fondling his genitals.*)
    I can't get it up!

CLEO. (*Sitting up, then caressing his neck.*)
    Don't be upset! That happens.

TONY. But it's never happened to me!

CLEO. (*Peeking over his shoulder at his groin.*)
    Even when soft and small, it has charm.
    And in that state, it allows me to admire
    that lovely pair of dangling plums
    and your beautiful black escutcheon.

EROS. (*Enters.*) My lord and my lady,
  I am sorry to interrupt,
  but I have important news from Rome.

TONY. What is it?

EROS. I have a letter from Octavian Caesar.

CLEO. Read it!

EROS. (*Reading.*) "From Octavian Caesar
  to Marcus Antonius:" (*Freezes.*)

OCTAVIAN. (*Appears.*)
  Senatus Populusque Romanus
  [The Senate and the People of Rome]
  declare that you, Marcus Antonius,
  are a public enemy.
  You have committed treason
  by presuming to give away
  what can never be given away,
  namely, Roman territory.
  Therefore,
  Senatus Populusque Romanus
  [the Senate and the People of Rome]
  have stripped you
  of all power and authority
  to rule the provinces of the East.

  As for Cleopatra, her illegal acceptance
  of the eastern provinces
  indicates her defiance
  and contempt for Rome

and is, in fact, an act of hostility
against Rome.
Therefore,
Senatus Populusque Romanus
[the Senate and the People of Rome]
declare war on Cleopatra,
Queen of Egypt. (*Disappears.*)

CLEO. Eros, is there more?

EROS. (*Animated.*) No more, my lady.

CLEO. Well, then, Eros, you may go.

> (EROS *exits.* TONY *and* CLEO *get
> out of bed and stand, wrapping
> themselves in separate sheets.*)

Well, what do you think?

TONY. I think it's serious.
What concerns me most
is that in every game
I've ever played with that boy—
whether darts or dice or cock fighting—
he's always emerged the winner.

CLEO. He won't win at war!

TONY. What makes you so sure?
He conquered me once,
in northern Italy,
after Julius Caesar's assassination.

CLEO. Italy is not Egypt!
    Besides, we'll fight Octavian Caesar at sea!
    The Egyptians are better seamen
    than the Romans,
    and we always win our sea battles—
    provided we have a large-enough fleet.
    We'll sail immediately to Athens,
    where we'll gather the largest armada
    the world has ever known
    since the Greeks sailed to Troy.

TONY. One thousand ships
    sailed to Troy.

CLEO. We won't need a thousand.
    Half that number will do.
    Caesar has at most
    two or three hundred boats
    at the Roman naval base at Brundisium,
    and they are small.
    With five hundred Greek ships of war
    and sixty Egyptian,
    we will easily be victorious.

TONY. Why would Caesar fight a sea battle
    in which he'd be so greatly outnumbered?

CLEO. He thinks our illicit love
    has made us impotent,
    however large our fleet!
    He clearly doesn't know
    what he's talking about!

TONY. He doesn't? *Really?*
    (*Then staring vacantly off into space.*)

CLEO. Really!
    We will have a decisive victory!
    And now, darling,
    give me a thousand kisses!

            (TONY *remains preoccupied and
            immobile.*)

                (*Fade-out.*)

                Scene 5

31 BCE, Athens, the port.

EROS. (*Enters.*) 31 BCE. Several months later.
    The port of Athens. (*Stands aside, almost im-
    mobile.*)

        (CANIDIUS *and* TONY *enter.*)

TONY. General Canidius,
    Caesar has agreed
    to let us choose the form of the fight,
    either at sea or on land at Actium.

            (TONY *pins up a large detail map
            that shows Actium with clarity in its
            context of Greece and Italy.   The*

map shows the northern promontory; the serpentine harbor; the southern promontory, where Actium is located; the Ionian Sea; and the heel of Italy, with Brundisium. He points to each place as he names it.)

Here is Actium,
on the western shore of Greece,
facing Brundisium,
in the heel of Italy's boot.
As you can see,
Actium is on the southern promontory.
Here is the mouth of the harbor,
and that's where we fight!

CANIDIUS. How many ships do we have?

TONY. Over five hundred.

CANIDIUS. And Caesar?

TONY. About two hundred fifty.

CLEO. (*Enters.*) We'll devour them
like a sea monster
swallowing minnows!

CANIDIUS. Commander,
it's not too late to change plans.
All your officers, including me,
still advise a land battle.

Marcus Antonius,
you are a splendid soldier,
a leader of soldiers,
the most experienced commander alive,
and your troops are disciplined
in land combat,
the finest army in the world.

TONY. How many troops
would we have?

CANIDIUS. Easily nineteen legions
consisting of eighty thousand infantry
and twelve thousand cavalry.

TONY. And Caesar?

CANIDIUS. The same.

TONY. So we'd be equal
in a land battle.

CANIDIUS. Equal in numbers,
but superior in skill.
So we would have the advantage.
Caesar's hoping for a sea battle.
He has a well-trained
and well-equipped navy
stationed at Brundisium.

CLEO. But our fleet is
twice as large!

CANIDIUS. Caesar's admiral
 is Marcus Agrippa,
 the finest of sailors!
 We have no one to match him.
 And Agrippa has a *real* navy.
 You can hardly call ours
 by that worthy name!
 We had to take simple countrymen
 gathered throughout Greece.
 Farmers and laborers,
 donkey drivers, reapers,
 and whatever riffraff—
 drifters and idlers—
 we could scrape up.
 And boys too young
 to join the regulars.
 Hardly any of them has set foot
 aboard a boat,
 let alone been trained to row
 or sail one.
 What kind of crews
 do you think they will make?
 And there aren't enough of them
 to man five hundred galleys.

 So, yes, we do outnumber Caesar . . .
 in *ships*.
 But even our ships trouble me.
 They are pretentious—
 built for size and show—
 and they are slow.
 Caesar's ships are swift, lightweight,
 and maneuverable.

Let Egyptians fight at sea.
Romans should fight on land.

TONY. My ability as a soldier
didn't help against the Parthians!

CANIDIUS. Have you forgotten Philippi
and your great victory there?
Besides, in Parthia
it wasn't so much the Parthians
as Winter and Famine that conquered us.
But it's summer now,
and when we reach Actium,
it won't yet be autumn.
And we have food and supplies
in abundance.
I beg you, fight on land.

(*He kneels before* TONY.)

Antoni, dux bone,
lucem redde tuae patriae.
[Marcus Antonius, dear leader,
bring back the light to your country.]

(*He   kisses* TONY*'s   hand   and
stands.*)

CLEO. (*Sarcastically respectful.*)
General Publius Canidius Crassus
has made a stirring speech,
but he's mistaken.
Agrippa may be a good sailor,

but I am better.
Furthermore, we have two excellent
Roman sea captains—Publicola and Sosius.

CANIDIUS. Speaking confidentially,
    my lady,
    Publicola and Sosius together
    are not half as good as Agrippa alone.

CLEO. That doesn't matter!
    Our massive ships will crush Caesar's
    like toys in a tub!
    And we have twice as many!
    It would be foolish
    to give up that advantage.
    Most important of all,
    Egyptians at sea are invincible!
    Invincible, Admiral Marcus Antonius!

CANIDIUS. My lady,
    except for the men
    on the sixty boats from Alexandria,
    we don't have Egyptian sailors! (*Pause*.)
    Marcus Antonius, it's up to you.
    How do we fight, on land or at sea?

CLEO. Oh, Tony, at sea!

CANIDIUS. (*Glowering at* CLEO.)
    With all due respect, my lady,
    I was addressing the general.
    (*To* TONY.) General Marcus Antonius,
    give me my orders!

TONY. General Canidius, man the ships!
     We sail for Actium!
     And at Actium we fight at sea!

          (*Fade-out.*)

          Scene 6

Almost two weeks later, Actium, Tony's ship.

EROS. Fair weather
     brought Tony and Cleo's armada
     to Actium in less than two weeks.
     Now at anchor
     (*Pointing to the map.*)
     in the serpentine harbor of Actium,
     we await the enemy ships.
     Cleo is captain of the Egyptian fleet
     and is aboard her flagship.
     Tony is captain of the Greek fleet,
     assisted by Captains Publicola and Sosius.
     The wind is blowing from the west.
     (*Stands aside.*)

CANIDIUS. The western wind
     is the prevailing wind in these parts.
     (*Pointing to the map.*)
     Caesar's fleet will fly from Brundisium,
     running before the wind,
     and be at Actium in no time.

TONY. Canidius, here's my strategy.
   Our ships are undermanned,
   and most of the men
   have never sailed.
   (*Pointing to the map.*)
   We'll have a front line of ships
   that'll drop anchor
   at the mouth of the harbor,
   just beyond the narrows.
   With no sails set, the wind from the west,
   and our bows pointed out to sea,
   the men need only pretend to row.
   When Caesar's fleet approaches,
   it won't be able to enter the harbor
   because we'll have plugged it up
   with our ships.

   When Caesar engages us,
   we'll spring our catapults
   and shower the enemy with missiles—
   balls of rock.
   We will, in effect, be fighting
   a land battle at sea!
   Our ships will be like floating fortresses,
   and Caesar will have to storm them.

CANIDIUS. That sounds
   like a good plan,
   but there's a problem with it.

TONY.   What's that?

CANIDIUS. Supposing the wind shifts?
     If an east wind comes up,
     our ships will turn,
     the bows facing the harbor,
     the sterns toward open sea,
     our backs to the enemy.
     It will look as if we are retreating.
     But because we won't be moving,
     Caesar will know we're at anchor.

CLEO. The wind isn't going to shift!
     And what if he knows we're at anchor?

CANIDIUS. Agrippa will realize
     we don't know what we're doing!
     And if that
     doesn't give him an advantage,
     I don't know what will!
     He will destroy our harbor-plug fleet.
     And as soon as we replace
     one string of ships with another,
     he'll destroy that one, too!
     Furthermore, the plug strategy
     will hem in the rest of the fleet
     and make it ineffective.
     Our advantage in numbers will be lost.
     To be effective,
     our fleet has to sail out to open sea,
     where we can take advantage
     of the great size of our ships
     and batter and ram Caesar's fleet.

TONY. Our ships won't be able
    to batter and ram,
    because Caesar's boats
    are as light as corks.
    Have you ever tried to ram
    a floating cork?
    No, Canidius,
    we have to use our galleys
    like land fortresses—
    ships anchored
    at the mouth of the harbor.
    If that strategy fails,
    we'll consider yours.

(Fade-out.)

Scene 7

A week later, Actium, Tony's ship.

(Pantomime accompanies the narration.)

EROS. Well, Caesar's navy
    sails from Brundisium,
    flies across the Ionian Sea,
    sees our ships at the mouth of the harbor,
    but sails right past them
    and the southern promontory.

    Our fleet does not advance.
    Caesar's admiral, Agrippa,
    correctly concludes

that our ships are at anchor.
Agrippa does not engage us
because the wind
is blowing so violently.

For four days the wind howls.
And then, on the fifth day,
the unexpected happens.
The wind dies, the boats are becalmed,
their bows pointing every which way.
Caesar's oarsmen
now relentlessly row toward us,
and three or four of his boats
surround each of our galleys at close range.
Both sides are now engaged.

As Tony predicted, it's like a land battle—
like the storming of a walled town,
with each of our ships a town,
and Caesar's boats the assailants.
We begin springing our catapults,
slinging the heavy shot,
each stone the size of an onion.
And the enemy starts hurling spears
on our decks
and showering us
with volleys of arrows.

TONY. (*Enters.*) How's the battle going, Eros?

EROS. Captain, so far
both sides seem equally matched.
But morale among the men is poor.

TONY. Why's that?

> (*Sounds of whirring and falling arrows and clanging spears; with each whir,* TONY *and* EROS *duck.*)

EROS. The men resent the Egyptians,
    especially Cleopatra.
    Romans and Greeks cannot accept
    an Egyptian as their leader—
    particularly a woman!
    It is humiliating—
    especially when the Egyptian woman
    is a better sailor than any of us!

TONY. Cleopatra herself
    expressed concern about this.
    And so did General Canidius.
    For that very reason, Canidius
    advised me to send Cleo home.
    (*Sighting something.*) Look there!
    One of our rowboats!
    What's a rowboat doing
    in the middle of a battle?

EROS. Captain Domitius
    commands that boat.

TONY. Domitius is one of my best officers!
    He's heading straight for Caesar's ship.
    What does he intend to do?
    Attack Caesar from a rowboat?

EROS. No, my lord, I don't think so.
　　　All the oars are going up.
　　　He's saluting Caesar.

TONY. It looks as if he's going
　　　to board the enemy ship!
　　　Caesar is surrendering
　　　to Domitius?

EROS. No, Captain,
　　　Caesar isn't surrendering.
　　　Domitius is defecting!

TONY. That's impossible!
　　　No officer has ever been
　　　more loyal than Domitius!

EROS. He's now boarding Caesar's ship.
　　　Domitius has gone over to Caesar!

TONY. Well, what of it?
　　　A man should have the freedom
　　　to fight for whichever side he wants,
　　　don't you think?

EROS. No, my lord!
　　　Defection is treason!
　　　And the sentence for treason is death—
　　　death by crucifixion.

TONY. There'll be no punishment
　　　so long as I'm in charge.

What good is a man to me
if his heart is with the enemy?
Let any man who supports Caesar
go over to him now,
taking all his belongings with him
. . . and Domitius's, too!

EROS. My lord, you are either
out of your mind . . . or more generous
than any man I've ever known.

TONY. Call it madness or generosity.
It's the right thing to do.

EROS. (*Narrating.*)
A northwest wind comes up.
The sixty Egyptian ships
have hoisted their sails!
(*Pointing.*) Look there!
It's Cleo's flagship!
She's running with her fleet
right through the thick of battle
and heading south toward open sea!

TONY. She's heading back to Alexandria!
She knows her presence is demoralizing,
so she's doing what's best.
Oh, noble queen!
You're confident of victory,
and you're letting us win without you!
She wants me to have all the glory!

EROS. Well, our men
        will certainly be happy
        to see her go.

TONY. Tell Captains Publicola and Sosius
        to sail our ships out to open sea,
        where they may fight unencumbered.
        As for me, I'm joining the queen!
        What good am I here?
        I'm a soldier, not a sailor.
        So the men will be happy
        to see me go, too.
        Lower a rowboat!
        I follow the queen!

EROS. Marcus Antonius,
        you cannot do that!
        Cleopatra can abandon us,
        but not you!
        You are our admiral and our leader.
        The sailors will be demoralized
        without you—
        and so will all the troops
        watching from the shore!

TONY. There's no cause for concern.
        We're going to win this battle!
        Didn't Cleopatra say we would?
        Didn't she say we were invincible?
        And my lady is never wrong!

        Let's go! Lower a rowboat!
        (*Shouting.*) Men,

Publicola and Sosius
are in charge now!
(*Wild-eyed.*) I have to get back
to Alexandria to make preparations
for our victory celebration! (*Exits.*)

EROS. (*To the audience, confidentially.*)
He's completely out of his mind!
At the height of battle,
when our men need
his guidance and leadership
and encouragement most,
this man, who never cared
about other people's liberty,
suddenly speaks of it
as if it were everyone's right—
and runs away himself!

What made Cleo leave?
Did she really think her presence
was demoralizing our fleet?
Was she really confident of victory
without her?
Did she want Tony
to get all the glory?
Or was she a coward
who simply ran away?
Or was she testing Tony's love—
to see whether he would stay
without her? (*Pause.*)
Or did she want to humiliate him
and destroy him at any cost? (*Contemplating.*)
Does it really matter

when the outcome's going to be the same?
He made all of Rome his enemy for her,
and look what she has done!

Tony deserts because she does!
His soul lives in her body
and goes wherever she goes!
So he abandons the men
who love him and fight for him
and are willing to die for him
to follow that woman
who began his destruction
and now is determined to finish it!

Well, our rowboat
comes up to Cleo's ship,
and we are taken aboard.
But we do not encounter Cleo.
Tony immediately
goes forward to the bow
and sits down by himself in silence,
either angry at Cleo
or too ashamed to see her.
And I suppose she feels the same way
about him.

> (TONY *enters as at the beginning
> —despondent, stone-faced, bare
> chested, and barefoot. He crouches
> and sits, head in hands.*)

During the whole three-day voyage
from Greece to Egypt,

Tony sat on the deck,
at the bow, not saying a word,
not eating, not drinking, not sleeping.
He just sat there.
And after we had anchored at Alexandria,
he went straight to his retreat,
where he continued to sit, head in hands.

(*Without fade-out, directly into the next scene.*)

Scene 8

30 BCE, Alexandria, Tony's retreat.

EROS. As at the beginning.
It is 30 BCE,
and we are in Tony's retreat.

>   (EROS *places a hand on* TONY*'s
>   shoulder.*)

Tony, it's Eros returning.
I've talked to the sailors.
They want to put up a fight,
even though
you won't be their commander,
and even though
there's no chance of winning.
The brave fleet
has already sailed from its moorings.
You can see the ships through the window.

(TONY *stands and, together with*
EROS, *looks out the window.*)

And look there! Caesar's ships
are beginning to enter the harbor.
The battle for Alexandria
has begun!

TONY. What's happening?

EROS. Our ships are engaging Caesar's.

TONY. No, they're not! Look!

EROS. All the oars are going up!

TONY. Just like Domitius at Actium!
    The Egyptian boats
    are not fighting Caesar.
    They're saluting him!
    They're going over to him!
    Look! The boats are turning!
    They mean to escort Caesar
    into the harbor! It's over!

EROS. Was this Cleo's doing?

TONY. No. She had nothing
    to do with Domitius's defection,
    and she had nothing to do with this.
    I gave the men the freedom
    to do as they wished,

     to fight for me or fight for Caesar.
     And they chose Caesar.
     Do you know, Eros,
     if every general in every war
     gave every soldier the choice of fighting
     for whichever side he preferred,
     I think wars would end sooner
     and with a lot less carnage.

EROS. My lord, forgive me,
     but I don't think many leaders
     would agree with you.

TONY. Eros, just think of it!
     The battle of Alexandria has been fought,
     and the great city has fallen
     without the loss of a single life!
     Have you ever heard of such a thing?
     As for me, it's all over.
     Death hunts down
     even the man who runs away.
     Everyone knows what a noble Roman
     ought to do under the circumstances.
     But I am not a noble Roman,
     never was.
     Well, at least I'm honest.
     Eros, do you want to see me
     dragged back to Rome in chains?

EROS. No, my lord, I couldn't bear that.
     I couldn't live to see that.

TONY. Then the time has come
  to do what we agreed you'd do.
  (*Spreading his arms.*)
  Eros, what do you see?

EROS. I see the man I serve and love.

TONY. You see before you a coward.

EROS. No, my lord, *that* I do not see,
  nor will I ever see.

TONY. I don't even have the courage
  to kill myself.
  So if you truly love me,
  run me through and end my misery.

EROS. No, my lord, I cannot do that.

TONY. Run me through, Soldier!
  That's an order!
  Do it!
  Now!

EROS. Well, give me your arm first.

   (TONY *and* EROS *clasp forearms,
   then embrace.*)

  Farewell, my lord . . . and my god.

TONY. Farewell, Soldier.
  Farewell, Friend.

(*They disengage.*)

Now position the sword
and get it over with!

EROS. I can't do it
while looking into the face
of the man I serve and worship.
At least turn away from me.

TONY. (*Turning and kneeling.*)
All right. I've turned. Strike!

EROS. Shall I strike now?

TONY. Yes. Strike home!

(EROS *falls on the sword.*)

EROS. Well, then, it's done!
And I escape the sorrow
of your death.

TONY. (*Turning. Crying out.*)
O noble Roman!

EROS. Farewell, my lord. (*He dies.*)

TONY. He could not kill me,
and yet so easily could kill himself.
So he's forcing me to do
what I lack the courage to do.

(*Remaining kneeling, he extracts the sword from* EROS *and aims it at his own midchest, then gazes toward heaven.*)

O Jupiter, solve me dementia!
[O Jupiter, release me from my madness!]

(*Hesitantly and reluctantly stabs himself.*)
I've missed the mark!
Missed my heart!
Where is the heart?
Not in the right place.
I am incompetent to the end!
And now Death,
like a very important person,
intends to keep me waiting.

(TONY *falls to the ground, moving about slightly, trying to rise.* CHARMION *enters quietly, surveys the scene with horror and astonishment, and goes to* TONY.)

Who's there?

CHARMION. Charmion,
the queen's attendant.
Marcus Antonius, she wants you
to come to her immediately.

TONY. Where is she?

CHARMION. In her tomb.

TONY. (*Lifting his head to face her.*)
    Her *tomb*?
    What's she doing there?

CHARMION. She saw
    the Egyptian fleet surrender
    and Alexandria fall.
    She wants to die now
    with you.

TONY. She makes better plans than I do.

CHARMION. But I see that you're wounded,
    my lord.

TONY. A miserable Roman
    tried to kill me
    but failed.

CHARMION. There are two litters outside
    waiting to carry us to Cleopatra.
    Here, let me help you.

> (*She wraps and ties her shawl
> around his chest wound and helps
> him to his feet.*)

TONY. We must hurry.
    I don't want her to get ahead of me.

(TONY *leans on* CHARMION *as they exit.*)

(*Fade-out.*)

Scene 9

A little later that day, Cleo's tomb.

(CLEO *is reclining on a bed of cushions.* TONY, *leaning on* CHARMION, *staggers in and collapses on the bed.*)

CLEO. (*Alarmed.*) Darling,
    what has happened?

TONY. The stupidest Roman of them all
    tried to kill me.

CLEO. Charmion, send for the surgeon!

TONY. Charmion, don't bother.
    It's too late for a surgeon. (*Pause.*)
    How cold I am!

> (CLEO *removes her sheer bed jacket, exposing her upper body, and draws him against her.*)

CLEO. Come to me, my soldier,
    come to my arms.
    I'll warm you up.

You've been far too long
from my embrace.

(*She cradles him.*)

TONY. (*Looking up at her.*) My love,
    don't grieve for me.
    If you can, save yourself.
    Don't tell Caesar that I killed myself.
    Tell him that *you* killed me,
    and he may show clemency,
    and you may be able
    to begin a new life.

CLEO. No. If there is a new life,
    I want to share it with you.

TONY. Darling, think only
    of our past happiness!
    During all our years together,
    there wasn't a moment
    when I didn't love you.
    What a life we've lived!
    You are the most famous
    and most powerful woman
    on the earth,
    and you belonged to me.
    We've had the love of the ages!
    And now it's ending.
    I'm dying,
    never to know your love again.

CLEO. Hush, Tony, don't say that!

TONY. Your love
    was worth more to me
    than fame and fortune.
    It was worth more to me
    than the world.
    Wife—my *only* wife!—
    hold me closer!

       (*She cradles him closer.*)

    I'm going away,
    but I'm afraid to go anywhere
    without you.

CLEO. Husband, don't be frightened.
    I'm here, and soon I'll be with you,
    never to part again.

TONY. O my love! One last kiss!

CLEO. One? I'll give you a thousand,
    and then a hundred more!

       (*She kisses him repeatedly as he
       dies, his arm dropping to his side.*)

    O my light, whose life alone
    has made it sweet for me to live!

    Sidere pulchrior ille est.
    [He is more beautiful than a star.]

(She kisses his lips, then sits up and talks to him.)

O Tony, in my entire life,
nothing has afflicted me so much
as this one brief moment
I've had to live without you.

(Standing and sobbing.)

What's left for me now?
To wait for Caesar—
in his mercy—
to lead me in chains
through the streets of Rome?

(CHARMION *helps put the bed jacket back on* CLEO.)

Charmion, when Caesar comes,
tell him that I asked
one favor of him—only one—
that Tony and I be buried together
in this tomb.

(CHARMION *nods.* CLEO *strokes* CHARMION*'s face, then kisses and embraces her.* CLEO *moves back toward the bed and notices a small covered basket by its side. She crawls into bed, picks up the basket, and removes the lid.)*

Figs! How strange!
Where did they come from?

CHARMION. A farmer brought them
    just before I went to bring
    Marcus Antonius here.
    He said it was a present for the queen.

CLEO. (*Removing and admiring a fig.*)
    There's no fruit
    Tony loved so much
    as figs.

> (*She takes a bite of the fig and then
> puts it back in the basket, noticing
> something else there.*)

What have we here?
An uninvited guest!
How did you know to come . . . now?
How did you know I needed you . . . *now*?
I didn't send for you.

> (*Holding up a small snake, then
> playing with it.*)

Now, wondrous creature,
come to my breast.

> (*She puts the snake to her breast.
> After a moment, she yelps.*)

Well done!

(She holds up the snake and talks to it.)

Do you know that evermore
you'll be famous?
Posterity will always remember you
and speak of you! *(Contemplating.)*
But what do you care for fame?
How ironic!
If the gods give fame,
whether you want it or not,
it is yours.
But if the gods do not give it,
however much you crave it,
it is never yours.

(She carefully puts the snake back in the basket, covers it, and sets it aside.)

There! Back in the basket with you
and back to your figs!

I see that Death is coming now
to lead me to my beloved;
so Death is not so dreadful after all.
I'm growing drowsy.
The viper's merciful drug is taking effect.
The pain of grief is leaving.
Lethargy creeps through every limb
and into my soul.
Tony! I see you through the mist.

Are you weeping?
Don't weep, my love!
I'm coming.

> (CLEO *dies, her head dropping
> onto* TONY*'s chest.* CHARMION
> *goes to the bodies. She kneels and
> carefully brushes aside hair from*
> CLEO*'s face. She gently strokes
> the face and weeps.*)

CHARMION. My mistress is dead.
   The Queen of Egypt is dead.
   Cleopatra is dead.
   (*Standing, continuing to weep.*)

> (OCTAVIAN *enters and gazes
> about in astonishment.*)

OCTAVIAN. What has happened?

CHARMION. Marcus Antonius is dead.
   Cleopatra is dead.
   Both by suicide.

OCTAVIAN. How did they do it?

CHARMION. He by his own sword.

OCTAVIAN. And she?
   I don't see any blood.

CHARMION. She died of overwhelming grief
    and a broken heart.
    She couldn't bear to live without him.

OCTAVIAN. Come now, Charmion,
    you are a hopeless romantic!
    How did she die?

CHARMION. She discovered an asp
    in a basket of figs
    and put it to her breast.

    (OCTAVIAN *examines* CLEO*'s breast.*)

OCTAVIAN. Ah yes, I see the fang marks!
    (*Pause.*) I am astonished to find myself
    filled with sorrow.
    Marcus Antonius was my partner
    in the world,
    and he was my brother-in-law as well.
    At Philippi he was my comrade in arms.
    To think he threw away the world . . .
    for *her.*

    (*Gazing toward heaven.*)
    O God of Love!
    The other gods acting together
    cannot do as much good
    as you, all by yourself, can do harm.

    (*Assuming an authoritative manner.*)
    Now I must put aside all sentiment
    and turn to affairs of state.

(CHARMION, *in one deft move,*
spreads a shroud over the bodies.
Then she stands aside immobile.)

Rome has won two great victories.
At Actium we destroyed
Marcus Antonius and Cleopatra's fleet.
Now Alexandria has fallen without a struggle—
without the loss of a single life.

(*Turning to the bodies, then back to the*
audience.)
No.
There was the loss of *two* lives.

(*Announcing.*)
I, Caesar,
first and foremost decree
that the kingdom of Egypt
is now a province of Rome.

I, Caesar, further decree
that Marcus Antonius and Cleopatra
shall have a royal funeral
here in this great city.
It shall be resplendent and magnificent.
And the Roman army present in the city,
along with all the people of Alexandria,
shall attend.

I, Caesar, finally decree
that Marcus Antonius and Cleopatra

shall be buried together in this tomb—
not so much because they wished it
as because it is impossible
to do otherwise.
They are tied together by bonds
stronger than any Roman law can break.

(*Pantomiming in a spellbinding manner.*)
Polo deripere lunam possim
[I can draw down the moon from the sky],

et possim et crematos excitare mortuos
[and I can bring the dead,
even the cremated, back to life]—
something only a god can do.
But there is something
Caesar or a god cannot do—
separate these two bodies
that contain one soul.
And as long as there are people
to tell the story,
Tony and Cleo will always be together.

(*Breaking the spell, announcing.*)
We shall prepare at once for the funeral!
And afterward we sail to Rome
(*With yearning and joy.*) and home!

(*Fade-out with trumpet fanfare,
during which* OCTAVIAN *imper-
ceptibly walks to and steps onto a
low platform on the side and upstage and faces the audience.*)

EPILOGUE

VENTIDIUS. (*Enters.*)
> Our play is over.
> As you have seen, Marcus Antonius
> was largely responsible
> for dealing the deathblow
> to the Roman Republic.
> After the death of
> Marcus Antonius and Cleopatra,
> Octavian Caesar
> became the sole and unopposed ruler
> of all the Roman provinces.
>
> In the year 27 BCE—
> three years after the death
> of Tony and Cleo—
> the Roman provinces became
> the Roman Empire,
> and Octavian Caesar became
> its first emperor.
>
> > (*Spotlight on* OCTAVIAN*'s head.*)
>
> His name became Augustus,
> which means Sacred or Revered
> or Divine,
>
> > (*A crown appears above* OCTA-
> > VIAN*'s head; his arms slowly rise
> > forward and laterally about forty-
> > five degrees, whereupon he freezes.*)

et Senatus Populusque Romanus
[and the Senate and the People of Rome]
declared that he was a god.

(*Blackout and grand trumpet fanfare.*)

THE END

ABOUT THE AUTHOR

HOWARD RUBENSTEIN is a physician and a writer. He was born in 1931 in Chicago, where he attended Lake View High School. He received a B.A. *magna cum laude* in 1953 from Carleton College, where he was elected to Phi Beta Kappa and Sigma Xi and won the Noyes Prize for excellence in ancient Greek. Rubenstein received his M.D. degree in 1957 from Harvard Medical School and was a practicing physician until 2000. He has published many scientific articles and essays. Now retired from the practice of medicine, he spends much of his time writing plays.